Executive Accountability in Southeast Asia
The Role of Legislatures in New Democracies and Under Electoral Authoritarianism

About the East-West Center

The East-West Center promotes better relations and understanding among the people and nations of the United States, Asia, and the Pacific through cooperative study, research, and dialogue. Established by the U.S. Congress in 1960, the Center serves as a resource for information and analysis on critical issues of common concern, bringing people together to exchange views, build expertise, and develop policy options.

The Center's 21-acre Honolulu campus, adjacent to the University of Hawai'i at Mānoa, is located midway between Asia and the U.S. mainland and features research, residential, and international conference facilities. The Center's Washington, D.C., office focuses on preparing the United States for an era of growing Asia Pacific prominence.

The Center is an independent, public, nonprofit organization with funding from the U.S. government, and additional support provided by private agencies, individuals, foundations, corporations, and governments in the region.

Policy Studies 57

Executive Accountability in Southeast Asia:
The Role of Legislatures in New Democracies and Under Electoral Authoritarianism

William Case

Executive Accountability in Southeast Asia:
The Role of Legislatures in New Democracies
and Under Electoral Authoritarianism
by William Case

ISSN 1547-1349 (print) and 1547-1330 (electronic)
ISBN 978-1-932728-88-0 (print) and 978-1-932728-89-7 (electronic)

East-West Center
1601 East-West Road
Honolulu, Hawai'i 96848-1601
Tel: 808.944.7111
EWCInfo@EastWestCenter.org
EastWestCenter.org/policystudies

The views expressed are those of the author(s) and not necessarily those of the Center.

Hard copies of publications in the series are available through Amazon.com.

In Asia, hard copies of all titles, and electronic copies of Southeast Asia titles, co-published in Singapore, are available through:

Institute of Southeast Asian Studies
30 Heng Mui Keng Terrace
Pasir Panjang Road, Singapore 119614
Email: publish@iseas.edu.sg
Website: http://bookshop.iseas.edu.sg

Contents

List of Acronyms

ACA	Anti-Corruption Agency
ARMM	Autonomous Region of Muslim Mindanao
BPK	Supreme Audit Agency
BROOM	Blue Ribbon Oversight Office Management
CMD	Christian and Muslim Democrats
COMELEC	Commission on Elections
CPP	Cambodian People's Party
DAP	Democratic Action Party
DPR	People's Representative Assembly
EAIC	Enforcement Agency Integrity Commission
Funcinpec	National United Front for an Independent, Neutral, Peaceful, and Cooperative Cambodia
GLC	Government Linked Corporation
Golkar	Functional Groups
GRC	Group Representative Constituencies
HRP	Human Rights Party

JAC   Judicial Accounts Commission

KAMPI   Partner of the Free Filipino

KBL   New Society Movement

KPK   Corruption Eradication Commission

MACC   Malaysian Anti-Corruption Commission

MCA   Malaysian Chinese Association

MIC   Malaysian Indian Congress

NBN   National Broadband Network

NEDA   National Economic Planning Authority

NEP   New Economic Policy

NMP   Nominated Members of Parliament

NPC   Nationalist People's Coalition

PAC   Public Accounts Committee

PAN   National Mandate Party

PAP   People's Action Party

PAS   Islamic Party of Malaysia

PBB   Star and Crescent Party

PCIJ   Philippines Center for Independent Journalism

PDAF   Priority Development Assistance Fund

PDI-P   Indonesia Democracy Party of Struggle

PKB   National Awakening Party

PKR   People's Justice Party

PKS   Prosperous Justice Party

PPI   Parliamentary Powers Index

PPP	United Party of Development
SRP	Sam Rainsy Party
UMNO	United Malays National Organization
UNTAC	United Nations Transitional Authority in Cambodia
ZTE	Zhong Xing Telecommunication Equipment Company

Executive Summary

In an influential study, Steven Fish and Matthew Kroenig argue that "overarching institutional designs" (i.e., presidential, parliamentary, and dual systems) tell us less about the prospects of a new democracy than does the particular strength of the legislature. Specifically, executive abuses are best checked where legislatures are powerful, generating horizontal accountability. Indeed, Fish and Kroenig suggest that with judiciaries and watchdog agencies weak in most new democracies, the legislature is the only institution by which accountability can be imposed. What is more, ordinary citizens are better informed by the robust party systems that strong legislatures support, fostering vertical accountability. In comparing Freedom House scores with their Parliamentary Powers Index (PPI), Fish and Kroenig show clear correlations, leading them to conclude that democracies are made strong by legislatures that are empowered.

In this monograph, their thesis about accountability and legislative power is tested in five country cases in Southeast Asia: Indonesia, the Philippines, Malaysia, Cambodia, and Singapore. Though many different kinds of regimes can be found in this part of the developing world, the politics of these countries can be broadly classified into two types. Indonesia and the Philippines are new democracies in which legislatures are formed through competitive elections. Malaysia amounts to a paradigmatic case of electoral authoritarianism in which civil liberties are truncated, while legislative elections, though competitive, are manipulated in a variety of ways. Cambodia and Singapore can also be understood as operating electoral authoritarian regimes, though their competitiveness is still more seriously diminished. The study's main aim, then, is to investigate which type of regime, a new democracy or electoral authoritarianism, better allows legislatures to check the executive.

Analysis begins by recounting the literature about the motivations of those who seek election to legislatures in developing countries. We find that in these conditions state power offers the surest means to the accumulation of personal wealth. Thus, in new democracies, though legislatures may be rated by the PPI as powerful, members are less motivated to check the executive than to capture state patronage. In Indonesia today, where political parties have remained reasonably resilient, members of the People's Representative Assembly cooperate through what have been variously conceptualized as rainbow coalitions and party cartels. They then share largesse across party lines through a system of legislative commissions. In the Philippines, though political parties are personalist and transient, most members of Congress join in support of the president's party, thus forming an outsized majority. As in Indonesia, members of Congress share patronage through a committee system.

> *Executives in new democracies gain legitimacy through popular election, but afterward avoid accountability in the legislature*

At the same time, with the executive in a new democracy having won some legitimacy by submitting to accountability on a vertical front through popular election, he or she is less in need of the legitimacy that is earned on a horizontal plane through legislative scrutiny. To illustrate these themes and the extent of the abuses that result, a particular instance of corruption is explored in each country case. In Indonesia, recent events involving the bailout of Bank Century and the legislature's reaction are rehearsed. In the Philippines, the dealings over a telecommunications contract offered to a Chinese company, FTZ, are recorded. These vignettes strengthen our conclusion that in new democracies, legislators are uninterested in rigorously checking the executive. At the same time, executives remain less tolerant of any checks that legislators might seek to impose.

By contrast, under electoral authoritarian regimes, though legislatures might be evaluated by the PPI as weak, a more exclusionary setting ensures that legislatures are better delineated between government and the opposition. Of course, legislators who join the ruling party or coalition may be just as geared to patronage as their counterparts in new democracies. But as those who join the opposition are barred from sharing in significant largesse, they are differently motivated when seeking election to the legislature. Accordingly, they confront the government fiercely over everyday policymaking and corrupt practices. In addition, they are galvanized by their quest to advance a transition toward more fully democratic politics. In Malaysia, then, where political parties have also been resilient, members of the opposition in Parliament engage in a variety of well-honed strategies to try to

Electoral authoritarian regimes better delineate and galvanize political opposition

hold the executive at least mildly accountable. Historically, they have made reasonably effective use of question time and debates. More recently, they have instigated some changes in bills that the government submitted concerning reform of the country's Anti-Corruption Agency and the police. On the other side, with the executive operating a regime type that falls short of the legitimation won through competitive elections, Malaysia's prime minister has remained more receptive to at least mild scrutiny in Parliament.

While Malaysia remains the best case of electoral authoritarianism in the Southeast Asian region, Cambodia and Singapore have operated baser versions of this regime type. Civil liberties are, thus, more sharply curtailed, and elections are more seriously manipulated. Even so, we see in Cambodia the extent to which members of the opposition Sam Rainsy Party have struggled to hold the government accountable in the National Assembly. And in Singapore, we see that because elections are so heavily manipulated, the government, in seeking greater legitimation, has sought to fabricate an opposition in the legislature through its Nominated Members of Parliament scheme. The kind of electoral authoritarianism that is practiced in these two countries is too closed to foster any meaningful checks on the executive. But, nonetheless, we find that even in these circumstances, at least some legislators are motivated to try.

Thus, in contrast to Fish and Kroenig, this study concludes that while legislatures are surely weaker under electoral authoritarian regimes than in new democracies, they better delineate the opposition, whose members try to use what powers they possess to check executive abuses. However, rather than leading to a fuller democracy, the accountability that results tends to strengthen authoritarian rule by adorning it with greater legitimation.

Executive Accountability in Southeast Asia:
The Role of Legislatures in New Democracies and Under Electoral Authoritarianism

The main aim of this analysis[1] is to show that executives may be held less accountable by their legislatures in new democracies than under electoral authoritarianism. To do this, it assesses legislative functioning under different regime types in Southeast Asia. In contrast to many other parts of the developing world constructed as regions, Southeast Asia is habitually, if incautiously, characterized as unbounded in its political diversity. To be sure, when compared with Latin America, southern and eastern Europe, and Northeast Asia, areas that have yielded to democratic "snowballing," and the Middle East and North Africa, which have remained almost uniformly authoritarian, Southeast Asia displays much pluralism. But the regimes of the major Southeast Asian countries considered in this study can be placed in just two categories: new democracies (in Indonesia and the Philippines, and Thailand until 2006), and electoral authoritarianism (in Malaysia, Cambodia, and Singapore, though in the latter two countries in more hardened forms). Thus, the pluralism of Southeast Asia's regime types is ordered, featuring a diversity that encourages comparison and a regional circumscription that applies analytical control, yet is restricted enough in the range of outcomes that meaningful generalizations can be made.

Southeast Asia offers a good setting, then, in which to gauge accountability in both new democracies and under electoral authoritarianism. Further, because all the country cases in this paper feature elected legislatures, we can examine across regime types the arenas that are most crucial for checking the executive. In a new study, Steven Fish and Matthew Kroenig (2009) demonstrate that the overarching institutional designs that are commonly investigated, whether presidential, parliamentary, or semi-presidential in form, tell us little about accountability: executives may abuse their powers amid any of these institutional medleys. What most matters, then, is the countervailing strength of legislatures.

However, our case studies from Southeast Asia show that while legislatures may be central to oversight, it is less the strength that they may possess than the preferences of their members that are pivotal. Thus, while legislatures have greater powers in new democracies like Indonesia and the Philippines, they better check the executive under electoral authoritarianism in Malaysia. Moreover, as this paradox deepens, we find that accountability is more effective at strengthening electoral authoritarian regimes than readying them for democratic change.

Legislative power is stronger in Indonesia and the Philippines, but more effective in Malaysia

In seeking explanation, the sections below address the organizational features of these countries' respective legislatures, the recruitment and motivations of their members, and the patterns and functioning, as well as the differentials in accountability, that result. The analysis concludes with a brief recommendation of how, in light of Southeast Asia's experience, accountability in new democracies might be raised.

Executives, Legislatures, and Variable Accountability

Analysts puzzle today over the failings of new democracies, as well as the rise of electoral authoritarianism. But in training their gaze on sundry institutional designs (e.g., Stepan and Skach 1993, Linz and Stepan 1996), they have found few answers. In new democracies, whether presidential, parliamentary, or dual systems are in place, a range of maladies flourish, especially executive abuses. When set within wider patterns of either elite-level fractiousness or mass-level tensions, these maladies can trigger collapse through military coups or popular uprisings. At the same time, electoral authoritarian regimes, though fronted by these same institutional systems, but frequently driven by single dominant parties, may more effectively restrain executives and order elite relations. And as they do this, coups and uprisings are better avoided.

Thus, under any institutional design, executives may be abusive or restrained in their conduct. Fish and Kroenig (2009: 5) caution that the attention given to "ideal-typical systems" amounts to a "blind spot in political science." What matters, they argue, are legislatures. Put simply, when legislatures are strongly endowed, executives are checked, and democracy's prospects are improved. But where they remain weak, abuses run rampant. And it is this failure to restrain the executive, argue Larry Diamond, Marc F. Plattner, and Andreas Schedler (1999: 1), as well as alienating other elites or disillusioning social forces, that most endangers democracy's "long-term survival."

In evaluating legislatures in some 160 countries, Fish and Kroenig have developed a Parliamentary Powers Index (PPI). The strength of legislatures is measured along four dimensions: a legislature's capacity (1) to influence the executive, (2) to remain autonomous from the executive, (3) to exercise sundry subsidiary powers, and (4) to access various resources. Fish and Kroenig contend that the switch from categorical to ordinal data that their index makes possible enables us to better identify and measure the locus of political power. To be sure, this scheme has drawn criticism over the weighting, clustering, and measurement of its nearly three dozen indicators (Melia 2010). But through statistical testing, the index still gains a "good result" for internal consistency (Melendez 2009). Hence, while sacrificing some precision, the PPI provides a usable framework for comparing the strength of legislatures across country cases.

Next, Fish and Kroenig argue that where legislatures are evaluated as strong, they can impose much horizontal accountability. Indeed, writes Fish (2006: 190), with judiciaries typically quiescent, "the legislature is the only agency at the national level that is potentially capable of controlling the chief executive." What is more, legislatures impose vertical accountability, fortifying the political parties that discipline politicians and collate policy platforms, which is essential for clarifying the appeals about which voters make judgments. Hence, in comparing their

Parliamentary Powers Index with Freedom House scores for civil liberties and political freedoms across countries, Fish (2006: 181) concludes that the "presence of a powerful legislature is an unmixed blessing for democratization."

By sharpening analysis down to one institutional arena, Fish and Kroenig relieve us of the ambiguities of overarching institutional designs. Even so, evidence from Southeast Asia shows that the legislative powers that they laud amount at most to an enabling factor. Where legislatures have been strong, their members have more often been motivated to join in abuses than to check the behaviors of executives. What is needed, then, for imposing accountability is a committed opposition. But, counterintuitively, opposition has been rarer in the new democracies of Indonesia and the Philippines than under electoral authoritarianism in Malaysia. Thus, as Guillermo O'Donnell (1998: 112) laments, while in new democracies accountability is by definition imposed on a vertical front through elections, it is notable on the horizontal plane for its "absence." Indeed, these dimensions may vary inversely. An executive in a new democracy, by gaining power through competitive elections, so enjoys a bloom of legitimation that he or she may often ignore the legislature, estimating that enough imagery of procedural rightness has already been fostered.

At the same time, legislators, having won their epic battles for democratic change, shed their ideological fervor and turn to everyday bargaining over policymaking. As they do this, they discover that the door to the treasure house of public resources has been thrown open. No longer guided by belief systems, then, the party vehicles that legislators operate fail to create a meaningful configuration of government and opposition. Instead, whether parties remain resilient but grow accommodative (as in Indonesia), repeatedly fragment and re-coalesce (as in the Philippines), or rotate through positions in the cabinet (as in Thailand during democratic periods), they avidly pursue the patronage with which their arena now hums. Executive abuses, far from being checked by the legislature, are rarely interrupted. When the legislature does impose accountability, it is principally to free up yet more public resources.

Where legislatures are powerful, members often join in on executive abuses

By contrast, under electoral authoritarianism, though multiparty elections are waged, vertical accountability is stunted by the manipulations that take place, as well as by the tight restrictions on civil liberties. Thus, under this regime type, though the single dominant party that typically operates it may more efficiently gain the compliance of citizens than do governments resorting to harder forms of authoritarian rule, the executive may seek to enhance his or her legitimation. Mild probing by the legislature may be tolerated, then, producing modest amounts of horizontal accountability.

In addition, Boix and Svolik (n.d.) show that by imposing some accountability, a legislature can strengthen power-sharing arrangements between the executive and his topmost allies in the cabinet, bureaucracy, and military. Specifically, by providing a "forum" wherein information about the volume, value, and distributions of public resources is clarified, the legislature helps resolve the "commitment and monitoring problems" that can corrode an authoritarian coalition. Joseph Wright (2008) shows, too, how legislatures, by posing a "credible constraint" on the executive's confiscatory behavior, can aid the "dictator" in enticing investors to expand the economy. Accordingly, even when unusually autocratic, an executive may "prefer a subservient legislature to no legislature at all" (Ziegenhain 2008: 15).

On the other side, while an executive benefits from horizontal accountability under electoral authoritarianism, a legislature more readily delivers it in these conditions than it does in a new democracy. With the legislature engaged in a two-tier game of momentous regime change and everyday policymaking (Schedler 2002), ideologies and party systems remain sharply delineated, hence confronting the government with a motivated opposition. But even as the executive continues to

> *Horizontal accountability can strengthen the executive even when it brings abuses to light*

share patronage among top-level allies and supportive legislators, the opposition's uncovering of these exchanges may only add to his or her legitimation, especially if followed by expressions of contrition and policy feints. Thus, in the absence of civil liberties and full electoral competitiveness, accountability serves mostly to strengthen the hand of the executive and the resilience of the electoral authoritarian regime.

William Case

But without alternatives, opposition legislators take the bait. However wrongly, they calculate that they can drive democratic transitions and policy changes by exposing the flows of largesse from which they and their constituents are barred. They strive mightily, then, to impose what accountability they can.

In sum, while strong powers might be enjoyed by a legislature in a new democracy, they may be parried by the executive and misused by its members. The legislature's influence over, or autonomy from, the executive creates scope not only to impose accountability in the ways anticipated by Fish and Kroenig, but also to extract state patronage. By contrast, though a legislature is far less endowed under electoral authoritarianism, such powers as it does possess may be more tolerated by the executive and more appropriately wielded by its members.

Accordingly, Fish and Kroenig may also have a blind spot. To be sure, their work addressing the extent of legislative empowerment marks an analytical advance. But to understand the variable levels of accountability that a legislature imposes, scrutiny must be extended to the calculations made by executives and the motivations of members. This study begins by reviewing the Freedom House scores and the Parliamentary Power Index ratings of the three key country cases. Indonesia's regime has been evaluated by Freedom House (2010) as "free" (with a score of 2 for political rights and 3 for civil liberties, on a scale in which 1 is free and 7 is not free). In the Philippines, though its status was revised downward by Freedom House from "free" to "partly free" in 2006 (with political rights slipping from 2 to 3 in the wake of allegations over electoral fraud), the institutions remain democratic in form. Further, the country's election in 2010 was widely adjudged to be fair, with electronic voting newly introduced to prevent manipulations. By contrast, though Malaysia's regime was evaluated as "partly free" in 2010 (4 for both political rights and civil liberties), freedoms of communication and assembly remain weaker than in the Philippines. And an election held there in 2008 that displayed greater competitiveness has been followed by renewed suppression of the media and opposition.

Thus, as would be expected, Indonesia's legislature has been gauged by Fish and Kroenig on the Parliamentary Powers Index as reasonably muscular at .56 (on a scale in which, contrary to Freedom House's, 1 is "most powerful" and 0 is "least powerful"). The legislature in the

Philippines has also been scored at .56. By contrast, the powers of Malaysia's legislature have been assessed as a puny .34.

However, though Indonesia and the Philippines are new democracies, earning their legislatures fairly high rankings on Parliamentary Power indices, their executives have tried generally to avoid horizontal accountability. And members of their legislatures have mostly been uninterested in imposing it, giving priority to colluding across party lines in pursuit of patronage. Meanwhile, in Malaysia, where electoral authoritarianism endures, major parties in the government and

High rankings on the Parliamentary Power indices do not equate with greater levels of accountability

the opposition remain firmly demarcated. Thus, when the executive is in need of legitimation and the opposition legislators are motivated to seek changes, however futilely, in both the regime type and policy outputs, greater levels of accountability have been attained.

Uneven Motivations and Varying Accountability

This section focuses more closely on how the motivations of legislators vary under different regime types. In advanced industrial democracies, Michael Laver and Kenneth A. Shepsle (1999: 283–84) contend that legislators are more dedicated to policymaking than mere office holding. Their evidence lies in the frequency with which minority governments prevail: "If the holding of office were the prevalent motivation, then we should never observe minority governments—the majority opposition parties could boot them out and secure the pleasures of office for themselves." Accordingly, Laver and Shepsle (1999: 294) blithely conclude that the cabinet should not be understood as merely "a sack of trophies to be divvied up among the 'winners.'"

But this implied availability of career options outside high political office is less true in the new democracies of developing countries. Lise Rakner and Nicolas van de Walle (2009: 115) observe, for example, that in sub-Saharan Africa, "the lack of economic development and weak private sectors have long led the ambitious to view politics as the most realistic channel for upward mobility. Political positions are often the route to business opportunities such as obtaining licenses of state contracts." In these conditions, Ellen Lust (2009: 129) writes succinctly that elections should be understood as a "business invest-ment." Accordingly, those who win legislative seats in these conditions are scarcely motivated to check the executive in hopes of producing better governance. Rather, they seek to collude with the executive in hopes that they might share in state patronage. And even where they try to impose accountability, legislators act less to keep the government honest than to replace it at the long trough of public sector resources.

Of course, under electoral authoritarianism, many legislators are similarly motivated. But without any transition to democracy having taken place, their parties remain more firmly demarcated as govern-ment- and opposition-aligned. In addition, where a single party gains dominance, Jason Brownlee (2007) shows that in fusing with the state apparatus, its monopolization of public resources and its distributions of patronage also help to define and strengthen the government's ranks. This dominant party also forges steep organizational barriers, distinc-tive sets of programmatic appeals, and solid bases of social support.

On the other side, for legislators in the opposition, their prospects for replacing the government through elections is slight. Hence, their best route to patronage involves defecting to the dominant party. But given the vast organizational and ideational gulf that they must cross, this would demand a price that many opposition members remain unwilling to pay for fear of losing their standing among political allies and social constit-uents. They also grow hardened by the distributions of patronage from which they and their constituents remain ex-cluded. Under electoral authoritarian-ism, then, the casual party-hopping and promiscuous clientelism that typically mar new democracies remain muted. Rather, legislators who remain firmly in opposition strive to hold the government accountable for its arbitrary controls and habitual misuse of public resources.

> *Casual party-hopping and promiscuous clientelism can be restrained by electoral authoritarianism*

Ellen Lust (2009: 125–26) remains skeptical, arguing that under conditions of electoral authoritarianism, which is equivalent to what she labels "competitive clientelism," legislators "have limited incen-tives to use their positions to challenge the regime." Rather, as in new democracies, legislators prioritize personal benefits: "perks...the glamour and prestige of being in parliament...cars, drivers, offices....immunity from prosecution." Meanwhile, those "most opposed to the regime....stay out of politics, instead channeling their efforts into civil society" (Lust, 2009: 128). Jennifer Gandhi and Adam Przeworski (2006) argue similarly that the legislature serves as an essential institutional "forum" through which "dictators" gain equilibrium by co-opting the opposition through policy concessions and rent sharing. And Andreas Schedler (2010: 71) states bluntly that within their small chambers, legislators are "easy objects of authoritarian control."

To be sure, these writers are correct in those cases where legislatures are formed under conditions of "hard" authoritarianism, such as New Order Indonesia, the Philippines under Ferdinand Marcos, and in Vietnam's single-party system. But under electoral authoritarian regimes like in Malaysia, Singapore, and Cambodia, dissidents do seek election to the legislature and gather resolutely in opposition. And much more striking than the scant patronage that is secreted to them are the heavy sanctions they incur for imposing accountability too effectively—sanctions involving their disqualification, financial ruin, and even exiling and jailing. Though these legislators possess far fewer mechanisms by which to impose accountability than they would in new democracies, they much more fully exploit what scope they possess. The country cases that follow explore the different motivations of legislators in new democracies and under electoral authoritarianism.

> *In Malaysia, Singapore, and Cambodia, dissidents are undeterred by the threat of heavy sanctions*

Regime Types, Party Systems, and Legislative Power

The People's Representative Assembly in Indonesia

In 1949, after mounting a revolution against Dutch colonizers, Indonesia won the independence that it had declared four years before. Although it eschewed the federalist system that the Dutch had counseled, the government adopted a semi-presidential form of democratic regime. However, with the armed struggle over independence raising the military's standing, and with social identities constructed locally as *aliran* strengthening but also polarizing the political parties that emerged, democratic politics succumbed to legislative deadlock and outer-island rebellions. Thus, after a single general election held in 1955, Indonesia fell victim to what Samuel Huntington (1991) characterized at the global level as democracy's "second reverse wave."

The regime was more deeply transfigured through extreme repression in 1965–66, producing a "triple hybrid" (Geddes 1999) form of authoritarian rule that persisted for three decades. Denominated by its ideologues as the New Order, it blended the features of personal dictatorship, military government, and single-party dominance. Indonesia's legislature, then, the People's Representative Assembly (DPR), though popularly elected, sizable in composition, and regularly convened, served up but thin legitimation for the state power concentrated in other parts of the political apparatus. Indeed, with most legislators cheaply bought off in the ways that Lust describes, their functioning was mocked through an infamous refrain of the "4Ds": *daftar, duduk, diam, duit* (register, sit, stay quiet, get paid).

But in 1998, after a year of severe economic shock and sustained student protests, capped by a murderous upsurge in the capital city of Jakarta, a complex bottom-up transition to democracy was unleashed (Aspinall 2005). As it neared a tipping point, many members of the legislature joined a procession of elite-level defectors, lending their weight to the transition's momentum. Foundational elections were held in 1999, followed by a series of measures that reorganized and fortified political parties, while equipping the DPR with vast new powers of oversight. Briefly, under new electoral laws, a form of proportional representation articulated by multimember districts was introduced. A partially closed list system was also used until 2008, enabling parties to rank their nominees. A "recall" mechanism was installed that permitted elected members who defied their party leaders to be replaced. And additional requirements over party memberships, Jakarta-based headquarters, and nationwide branch systems effectively barred independent candidates and regional entities from the legislature. In these ways, respective party leaders strengthened their hand over nominations and resources.

Thus, amid a constellation of many dozens of new parties, a protean core of five to nine major vehicles has persisted, several of which, including Golkar (Functional Groups) and the PDI-P (Indonesia

Democracy Party of Struggle), are largely secular carryovers from the New Order period, while several others are moderately Islamic. To be sure, these vehicles have been distorted by internal autocracy and personalism, the factionalism that results, and the more urgent pursuit of patronage than any programmatic content (Ufen 2006, Mietzner 2008). In recent years, most all of them have lost popular support, threatening a process of "de-alignment" (Tomas 2010: 146–47). However, they have not yet dissolved in the ceaseless splintering and recrudescence that have characterized their counterparts in the Philippines and Thailand during democratic periods. In different interpretations, the emergence of this reasonably stable configuration, amounting to what Dan Slater (2004) conceptualizes, though overstates, as a "party cartel," has been attributed to the institutional rules canvassed above, as well as to a unique path dependence that originated in the New Order (Mietzner 2008), structural continuities in elite-level networking (Slater 2004), and cultural systems that deepen the social roots of parties, yet have come over time to favor consensual interactions between leaders (Sebastian 2004).

Next, to give the DPR new powers of oversight, a system of commissions (*komisi*) was set up. Dedicated to particular policy areas like finance, security, transport, and agriculture, eleven such commissions, supported by numerous subcommissions, have provided members with a mechanism for evaluating executive appointments and performance, as well as approving legislative proposals. These commissions have been supplemented by a range of standing and special committees. In this context, Fish and Kroenig (2009: 316) conclude that in Indonesia "the legislature is a fairly weighty institution. It has some influence over the executive, including the ability to interpellate and investigate executive branch officials. It has a fair amount of institutional autonomy....It exercises a number of specified powers, and it has considerable institutional capacity." Vishnu Juwono and Sebastian Eckardt (2008: 293) concur, arguing that the DPR "has gained substantial powers to scrutinize and to react to initiatives and policies proposed by the executive."

The Philippine Congress
Democratization preceded independence in the Philippines, with US colonial officials supporting presidential institutions, a two-party system,

and regular elections during the 1930s. The Nacionalista Party, having been formed in 1907 to advance independence, and the Liberal Party, having broken from the Nacionalistas after the Second World War, ordered elite-level competitions for control of the presidency and the Congress, and access to the modestly built state apparatus. After the Second World War, independence was granted and democratic politics persisted for nearly three decades.

But if democracy lasted longer in the Philippines than in Indonesia, the interests of most citizens remained unaddressed by Congress. The Nacionalistas and the Liberals, as disembodied elite-level vehicles, possessed nothing like the *aliran* bases that their counterparts drew upon in Indonesia. President Marcos, elected in 1965 after having switched from the Nacionalistas to the Liberals to gain nomination, imposed martial law in 1972 in order to keep his grip on state power beyond the two-term limit that he faced. Marcos first closed but then partially reconvened Congress. However, as his elections and referenda remained ad hoc, the new ruling party that he formed, the New Society Movement (KBL), generated scant legitimation. Indeed, the Nacionalistas and the Liberals mounted boycotts, further diminishing the meaningfulness of the contests that were held, but also that of their own party labels and apparatuses.

In 1983, however, the assassination of Marcos's chief rival, Senator Benigno Aquino, created pressures for democratic change. And three years later, Marcos's efforts to steal an election triggered the popular upsurge and elite-level defections that were heralded as "people power" (Thompson 1995). Under a new constitution, Congress was revitalized, with more than 200 representatives in the lower house standing for election every three years in single-member districts. Half of its 24 senators ran at the same time for six-year terms in a nationwide election. Term limits were also put in place, with representatives eligible for three consecutive terms and senators for two. In addition, through a mixed electoral system that was later introduced, 20 percent of the seats in the legislature were to be reserved for party list candidates representing popular sectors that were traditionally viewed as marginalized.

Since re-democratization, candidates for Congress have continued to find party labels and nominations helpful at election time. Parties swear in members and recruit campaign volunteers and canvassers. But as they lack cultural underpinnings, constitutional basis, public funding, and any organizational scaffolding at the branch level, parties have suffered far more from tactical de-alignment and re-coalescence than have their counterparts in Indonesia. Hence, these vehicles flourish only briefly, revved up by presidential candidates during campaigning, then by elected presidents during their single terms. To spur their respective campaigns, Fidel Ramos formed a new party, Lakas (Strength); Joseph Estrada created Laban (Fight); and Gloria Macapagal-Arroyo forged KAMPI (Partner of the Free Filipino). In the most recent presidential election held in 2010, winner Benigno Jr., the son of Benigno Aquino, reenergized the Liberal Party, encouraging defectors from a split four years earlier to, in their own phraseology (interviews 2010[2]), "come home." At the same time, Aquino's main opponent, Senator Manuel Villar, revived the Nacionalistas, only to watch the party fade upon his defeat. After presidential elections, representatives rushed to join the new House majority, a scramble that they and their staff officials colorfully describe in interviews (2010): "Changing parties is like changing pants."

Nonetheless, Congress has been given powers of oversight through an elaborate committee system in the House of Representatives and the Senate that shadows the US legislature. The first few weeks after a new legislature has been elected are spent apportioning leadership positions and memberships. Among the representatives, postings to such committees as Appropriations, Ways and Means, Banking, and Games and Amusements are among the most coveted. But accountability is more explicitly imposed by the Oversight, Good Government, Ethics, and Justice

> *In the Philippines, an elaborate committee system that shadows the US legislature possesses formal powers of oversight*

committees. Indeed, it is in the lower house's Committee on Justice that an impeachment complaint is first taken up, and any recommendation for an impeachment trial is then acted on by the Senate. Thus, no matter how feeble party loyalties might be, Fish and Kroenig (2009: 535) conclude as follows:

> Congress has significant, albeit not vast, authority. Its ability
> to influence the executive branch includes powers to impeach

the president, interpellate and investigate the government, and review the president's ministerial appointments. It has some degree of institutional autonomy, as evidenced by the president's lack of decree, dissolution, and gate keeping authority.... It has substantial institutional capacity.

The Parliament of Malaysia

At the time of independence from Britain in 1957, Malaysia, like Indonesia and the Philippines, operated a democratic regime. But given its lineage, Malaysia's democracy was elaborated along parliamentary lines, featuring single-member districts and plurality rule. It also acquired a ceremonial Senate, as well as a Council of Rulers, by which to accommodate hereditary sultans. Throughout the 1960s, though the prime minister sometimes behaved arbitrarily, his party, the United Malays National Organization (UMNO), gained ascendancy and politics remained reasonably democratic.

But during the second reverse wave, while democracy was felled in Indonesia by conflicting social *aliran*, deadlocked political parties, and a surging military, then dashed in the Philippines amid the vacuity of parties and severe presidential abuses, it was undermined in Malaysia by communal rivalries. Through policies of overseas labor recruitment, the British had forged a "divided" society, pitting "indigenous" Malays against "non-Malay" communities, the latter a stigmatized group composed of local Chinese, Indians, and others. The moderate but paramount UMNO led a multiethnic coalition whose partners included the Malaysian Chinese Association (MCA) and the Malaysian Indian Congress (MIC). But in a general election held in 1969, it was confronted on one flank by the Islamic Party of Malaysia (PAS) and on the other by new opposition vehicles, most notably the Democratic Action Party (DAP). These parties appealed, respectively, to the Malays and the Chinese. With the Malay vote now split between UMNO and PAS, the fortunes of the DAP surged, triggering an ethnic upheaval in Kuala Lumpur known as the May 13th incident. Emergency rule was declared and Parliament closed, then partially reopened, with politics equilibrating in electoral authoritarianism.

Under this regime type, characterized by severely truncated civil liberties and manipulated but multiparty elections, UMNO sought to reenergize its Malay social base. In brief, it tightened the institutional grip that it had earlier possessed, more deeply subordinating the MCA and the MIC. For a time, it also absorbed all of the opposition parties, save the DAP, into its coalition, which was rebadged as the Barisan Nasional (National Front). Next, UMNO fused with the state bureaucracy, with top offices in the party and state apparatuses now correlating closely. Indeed, Malaysia's prime ministership is treated, at least informally, as an ex-officio position held by UMNO's president.

As UMNO turned its hand next to restructuring electoral and parliamentary procedures, its president, Tun Abdul Razak, doubling as prime minister, famously intoned that "so long as the form [of democracy] is preserved, the substance can be changed to suit conditions" (Zakaria 1989: 349). Thus, in preparing for elections, UMNO's president, after conferring with Barisan chief ministers in Malaysia's various states, selected his party's parliamentary and state assembly candidates. He also vetted the candidates chosen by his Barisan coalition partners. At the same time, UMNO retained the single-member district system that the British had installed, though it now greatly exaggerated a principle of rural weighting that favored Malay voters—so much so that gross

Malaysia's steeply bipolar social structure has given rise to single-party dominance

malapportionment, elaborated with fanciful gerrymandering, grew entrenched. The government benefited further from the plurality rule, as the popular majorities of 50–60 percent that the Barisan customarily won were now amplified into extraordinary two-thirds majorities in Parliament, which was the amount necessary for freely amending the constitution. Thus, in striking contrast to the cartelization of parties in Indonesia and the transience of those in the Philippines, Malaysia's steeply bipolar social structure gave rise to single-party dominance.

Finally, in reconfiguring the Parliament in which elected legislators would gather, UMNO sought to weaken the body's capacity for oversight. As a condition for its reopening in 1972, the government demanded swift ratification of a series of "draconian" amendments; in particular, new sedition laws that prohibited any questioning of ethnic Malay "special rights" (Crouch 1996: Chapter 5) were enacted. Legislators were given no immunity against these laws, leaving them vulnerable to arrest. More than just restricting the deliberations necessary for legislative oversight, the government had dulled the competency of parliamentarians to debate even those policy areas that remained open. Specifically, in rigidly invoking its Standing Orders, the government had blocked the installation in Parliament of any real committee system. Legislators were hindered, then, in developing policy expertise and monitoring government performance. They found it even more difficult, of course, to mount any motions of no confidence. In this context, Fish and Kroenig (2009: 428–29) conclude that Malaysia's Parliament "has few…means to influence the executive….The legislature does not regularly question executive branch officials….In practice, a vote of no confidence would be unthinkable…The legislature has some institutional autonomy [but] its institutional capacity is slight."

In a rare scholarly analysis of Malaysia's legislature, Noore Alam Siddiquee (2006: 47–48), concurs, writing that it has not been able to assert itself as "a powerful watchdog on the functions of the executive….Despite all its trappings and grandeur, the Parliament in Malaysia is no more than a rubber stamp in the hands of the Cabinet." Fish and Kroenig thus award Malaysia's legislature with a lowly score on their Parliamentary Powers Index, mentioned above.

> *Malaysia's parliament is often dismissed as 'a rubber stamp in the hands of the Cabinet'*

Legislative Recruitment and Incentive Structures

Representatives in Indonesia

In Indonesia, most of the persons seeking entry to the legislature possess middle-class status derived from modest entrepreneurism, trade professions, civil society organizations, or religious groups. However, analysts have also tracked a sharp "rise in business representation" (Bima 2006) and, hence, a "great number of rich people" (Ziegenhain 2008: 119) in the DPR today. Indeed, after claiming the chairmanships of key parties such as Golkar and PAN, "wealthy entrepreneurs" have shoved aside "more professional and committed…party cadres, [and] dominated the corridors of power in Parliament" (Tomas 2010:

148). The conduits between Indonesia's ramshackle but still bountiful state apparatus and its grasping but nascent business class now teem with legislators seeking to deepen their personal stakes and hasten their mobility by gaining access to public resources.

In seeking election to the DPR, candidates have had, until recently, to gain high ranking on a party list. To obtain this, they usually had to make party "contributions," yet fund their own campaigns (Ufen 2006: 22). If successful in their bid, they also had to repay their selectors and canvassers before beginning to generate personal returns. Because of these demands, they have found little in the DPR's plenary sessions

> *Indonesia's legislature teems with operatives seeking access to public resources*

to occupy them (Sherlock 2010: 167–68). Though the full chamber occasionally radiates with debate, its mostly operates perfunctorily, either hosting ceremonial rites or duly ratifying legislation, most of which originates with the executive. Rarely does this body summon officials for questioning. Never has it vetoed legislative proposals. Those who are recruited to the DPR focus their quest for largesse on the more meaningful subsystem of commissions and committees.

Congressmen in the Philippines

Except during the martial law period under Marcos, Congress has operated continuously in the Philippines since the introduction of the constitution in 1935. Throughout this period, just as Lust would expect, those seeking entry to the legislature have been as motivated as their counterparts in Indonesia to gain access to public resources. As Paul Hutchcroft (2007) recounts, in the Philippines "special access to the state apparatus has been the major avenue for private wealth accumulation."

But in the Philippines, much more than in Indonesia, the social lineages and recruitment patterns of legislators possess historical grounding and continuity. The origins of the Philippine sociopolitical structure lie in the colonial period, where the interests of Chinese *mestizos* were promoted by the Spanish and consolidated by provincial land holdings and political positions under the Americans. Indeed, *mestizos* were found "useful" by US officials in extending their administrative reach across the archipelago (Hutchcroft 2000). After entrenching family networks through governorships and mayoralties, *mestizos* treated their local bases as springboards from which to launch their kinship groups—popularly characterized as clans or dynasties—into congressional positions, where they extracted state patronage through "booty" capitalist dynamics (Hutchcroft 1998).

> ***Political clan members have used their congressional seats to perpetuate 'booty' capitalist dynamics***

These patterns were disrupted by Marcos, who sought to strengthen state power and centralize patronage, and to promote new sets of cronies. He also locked out the traditional clans by closing Congress and reopening it in truncated form. But after re-democratization in 1986 and the full restoration of Congress, many clans like the Aquino-Cojuangcos of Tarlac, the Osmenas of Cebu, and the Lopezes of Negros plotted their return to legislative seats. In the less settled circumstances after Marcos's demise, they were joined in their pursuit by new clans, such as the Pimenteles of Cagayan de Oro and the Guingonas of Misamis; the new rich of Manila, such as real estate tycoon Manuel Villar; and a fringe of star athletes and media celebrities.

In this context, while two out of three members of the 12th Congress (2001–2004) were identified as members of political clans, the rate rose to 75–80 percent in the 13th and 14th Congresses (Coronel 2004, GMA NewsTV 2009a). Typically, after reaching the limit of three consecutive terms, a representative would pass the seat to a close relative, then repair to a provincial or municipal post in his or her place of origin. After a requisite single term, the former representative could return to the lower house or even seek entry to the Senate.

Aware of the poor imagery projected by clan dynamics and evasions of term limits, especially amid weakening patterns of social deference, a bill was proposed in the legislature to enforce the 1987 constitutional ban on political dynasties. But with congressmen also keenly aware of the usefulness of public resources for bolstering their private fortunes, they have let the bill languish for a decade. Indeed, they increasingly equip their family scions with advanced degrees in business administration, often from leading American institutions, in order to anchor their enterprises more deeply.

Despite the deeper erosion of party identification in the Philippines than in Indonesia (Ufen 2006), candidates for the House of Representatives still seek party nominations and signifying banners. As in Indonesia, upon winning nomination, they must obtain their own funds to hire the canvassers and vote buyers who will drive their campaigns. For candidates of established political clans who are confronted in elections by feisty upstarts, they tend to recruit the goons and gunmen who feature so disastrously in Philippine political life. In a frequently cited admission, Jose de Venecia, a former House Speaker who fell out with President Arroyo, disclosed the source of funding: "It's the drug lords and the gambling lords...who finance the candidates. So, from Day One, they become corrupt. So, the whole political process is rotten" (Hutchcroft 2008, quoting Bordadora 2007).

Hence, on their entry to the lower house, representatives must vigorously seek patronage that, in adopted American parlance, is widely derided as pork barrel. As discussed later, discretionary funds are allotted each year to those representatives who join the House majority in supporting the president's choice for the House Speakership. Still more funding can be secured by gaining positions on key committees that open conduits to the bureaucracy. Plenary sessions meet more regularly and bear greater significance than in Indonesia's DPR. But committees provide similarly productive arenas for mediating patronage distributions.

Parliamentarians in Malaysia

In Malaysia, UMNO candidates for Parliament were historically recruited from the civil service, forming cohorts that were mostly made up of retired bureaucrats and school teachers. But beginning in the 1980s, these groups were eclipsed by small business people. Legislators grew even more strongly motivated than in Indonesia to advance their business interests, responding to a distinctive set of public policy incentives. Specifically, after reopening Parliament in 1972, the government unveiled a large-scale program of ethnic "reverse discrimination," broadly labeled the New Economic Policy (NEP) (Gomez and Jomo 1999: Chapter 3). Seeking to reenergize the loyalties of the Malays who had abandoned it in the 1969 election, UMNO christened the community as "sons of the soil" (*bumiputra*), therein celebrating indigenous birthright. It also enlarged the state apparatus with many new agencies and services that gave advantages to the Malays through quotas on university placements, managerial positions, business licensing, lending, and equity stakes. It was for this reason, then, that Parliament's powers of oversight were initially restricted through "draconian" constitutional amendments, nearly silencing non-Malay legislators who had grown alienated over their constituencies' "second-class" citizenship.

Accordingly, many ambitious Malays, in seeking access to public resources through the NEP, quickly realized that gains could most efficiently be made by joining the dominant UMNO, climbing its party apparatus, and winning nominations for parliamentary or state assembly elections. What is more, the party's resources relieved its candidates of having to independently solicit canvassers and vote buyers. To the contrary, its candidates in key constituencies have counted on top party officials, often serving as government ministers, to weigh in personally with on-the-spot development grants while campaigning locally on their behalf.

Ambitious Malays quickly saw the benefits of climbing the UMNO party apparatus and entering Parliament

When successful, UMNO candidates find that, as in Indonesia, cabinet posts are most lucrative, with many ministers acquiring vast private assets (Pepinsky 2007). Even ordinary government backbenchers learn that they can secure handsome returns. Indeed, given Malaysia's higher developmental level and more sophisticated corporate scene, many winning candidates have eschewed crude payments from executive agencies, opting instead to use their seats as high-tension springboards to more profitable state contracts and credit. In this way, an exclusive social category of businesspeople has emerged among the *bumiputra*, informally known as "UMNO-putra" (Mauzy 1993: 118).

Numerous studies have disclosed the intimacy between government and business (e.g., Jesudason 1989, Gomez and Jomo 1999) in Malaysia, prompting James Chin and Wong Chin Huat (2009: 83) to declare that "patronage politics is hard-wired into the UMNO and [Barisan] machinery." A good illustration of what motivates government legislators can be found in a case that came to light in 2006. A UMNO parliamentarian, whose company was caught smuggling illegally harvested timber from Sumatra into Malaysia, was reported to have asked customs agents to "close one eye" (Beh 2006). In defending himself before Parliament and the media, he remarked, "I don't know whether my company was involved. Maybe yes, maybe no. If yes, so what? Why can't an MP take care of his own interest?" It can be concluded from readily observable incentives, then, that legislators in Malaysia's ruling coalition, like their counterparts in Indonesia's party cartel and the Philippine House majority, have been largely motivated by patronage in seeking entry to Parliament.

However, the legislature in Malaysia is also distinguished by committed opposition, whose members are motivated differently. Galvanized by aspirations to change the political regime and policy outputs, most opposition legislators remain untempted, at least at this pre-democratic juncture, by the prospect of patronage. Of course, they are deterred from adopting strongly anti-system strategies, as their legislative positions provide reasonable salaries, professional

> *Most opposition legislators in Malaysia remain untempted by patronage*

status, some organizational autonomy, and mobilizing opportunities. Recalling Lust (2009), opposition provides a measure of legitimacy and is a reason for any autocratically minded executive to consent to a legislature's formation. But the fact that opposition legislators usually eschew more substantial allurements is demonstrated by the infrequency with which they defect to the Barisan, a route that is narrowed, but not closed, by the government's ethnic Malay weighting. Indeed, UMNO usually welcomes those who seek to defect to some party component within its ruling coalition, even those who had earlier left but wish to reenter. But as this study reveals, most opposition legislators prefer to remain in opposition, resolutely using the tools that have been ceded to them to check the executive.

Legislatures and Executive Checks

Low Accountability in Indonesia

Fish and Kroenig are right in stating that Indonesia's DPR possesses reasonably strong powers for imposing horizontal accountability. But its members have generally underutilized or even misused their lever-age. As Edward Schneier (2004: 25) dryly observes, though the DPR may possess "the essential tools of oversight…how effective they are is another question." To be sure, the legislature meets resistance from the executive. When a democratic transition ushers in a regime that earns legitimation through vertical accountability, its presidents have sought to avoid horizontal accountability. Indeed, Indonesia's second

Even when the DPR imposes accountability, its members seek political gains

president after transition, Abdurrah-man Wahid, in citing his office's pre-rogatives, responded through a minion during interpellation by the DPR that he answered to no one over his cabinet selections (Ziegenhain 2008: 141). In another instance, he notoriously de-rided the DPR as "no different from a kindergarten." His successor, Megawati Sukarnoputri, also tried to keep her distance from the legislature, though she remained less out-wardly contemptuous than aloof. The current president, Susilo Bam-bang Yudhoyono, when summoned by the DPR for questioning, has each time deflected requests, either citing the popular mandate he ob-tained through the rule changes that led to his direct election in 2004 and 2009 or contriving scheduling conflicts.

While usually unfocused, the DPR has occasionally responded by exercising oversight. Indeed, its members grew so vexed over Abdur-rahman's behavior that they finally impeached him. They also grew "eager to find faults and irregularities" in Megawati's administration, unearthing scandals and threatening investigations (Ziegenhain 2008: 182). And they have several times confronted Yudhoyono. After Megawati lost to Yudhoyono in the 2004 presidential election, she ap-peared to break with the party cartel by refusing to accept a cabinet post for the PDI-P, professing to be "in opposition." After her second defeat in 2009, the PDI-P supported Golkar in mounting what Ste-phen Sherlock (2010: 171) depicts as a "textbook example of effective parliamentary oversight of the executive." In brief, Yudhoyono's finance minister, Sri Mulyani, and his vice-president, Boediono, a former gov-ernor of the central bank, had organized a bailout during the previous year's global financial crisis for a stricken local institution, Bank Cen-tury, fearing the impact of its collapse on the country's financial sector.

But disbursements soon swelled to four times what had been autho-rized by the DPR (*Asia Sentinel,* September 4, 2009). In November, the chairman of the Supreme Audit Agency (BPK), Hadi Purnomo, pronounced the bailout imprudent and illegal. Rumors circulated that some of the funding had found its way into Yudhoyono's reelection campaign. In this context, legislators from the PDI-P and Golkar de-manded that the DPR set up an inquiry over whether to investigate Sri Mulyani and Boediono. Their call was taken up by members of two Muslim parties, the United Party of Development (PPP) and the Prosperous Justice Party (PKS), which, like Golkar, also held govern-ment cabinet posts. Two new parties, Gerindra and Hanura, having for the first time won seats in the DPR in the 2009 election, also joined, enabling an inquiry to proceed.

As noted above, after a democratic transition has taken place, just as executives resist horizontal accountability, so too do legislators lose their motivation to impose it. What incentives, then, drove legislators in these instances to check the executive? In the case of Abdurrahman's impeachment, Slater (2004: 67) contends that the impe-tus was less the president's executive abuses and policy ineptness than his failure to meet the expectations of party leaders over ministerial appointments, which can be

Abdurrahman was impeached principally for failing to dole out appointments to party leaders

summed up in the catchphrase, "We give you the presidency, you give us the cabinet." Similarly, Ziegenhain (2008: 182) argues that because early in Megawati's tenure she had cold-shouldered the DPR when appointing ministers, the investigations mounted against her were "exploited for political gains." Once Megawati relented, relations be-tween the executive and legislature soon settled. During Yudhoyono's first term as president, he remained similarly obliging, mostly keeping the DPR at bay. Accordingly, Megawati's confronting him seemed less ideological than personal, with her bitterness having arisen over her second electoral defeat by Yudhoyono. Indeed, though soundly beaten, she refused to concede, instead demanding an inquiry over cheating. However, her husband, Taufik Kiemas, and her daughter, Puan Maharani, who as top-level PDI-P officials lead the party's "pragmatic group," have sought reconciliation with Yudhoyono and reentry to the cabinet (*Jakarta Globe*, 2010). Its members in the DPR have continued to participate vigorously in the commission system.

In the Bank Century case, we observe that it was only after business firms controlled by the chairman of Golkar and onetime coordinating minister for economy, Aburizal Bakrie, had been pressed over tax evasion by Sri Mulyani that the party's legislators, together with those from the PDI-P, began to call for an investigation. Bakrie had evidently been antagonized also by a number of other Finance Ministry decisions that had negatively affected his company's stock market valuations and asset acquisitions (von Luebke, 2010: 85). Further, we note that Purnomo, the BPK official whose report had given the DPR sanction for the proceedings, had himself been earlier dismissed as head of the tax office by Sri Mulyani for corruption. The PPP and the PKS, in defecting from the government to join the fray, sought to weaken the cabinet's technocratic elements. And the new parties, Gerindra and Hanura, sought avidly "to tarnish the government's anti-corruption image" (von Luebke, 2010: 85).

In driving the inquiry onward, Bakrie has been portrayed as "hoping to settle a score with his former cabinet rival, Sri Mulyani" (*The Economist*, 2010). Indeed, with analysts observing that the reformist commitments of Sri Mulyani and Boediono had "earned many enemies" among business elites, the DPR was widely interpreted as "trying to use the inquiry to oust the two technocrats" (*South China Morning Post*, 2010a). Von Luebke (2010: 84–85) finds a "display of hypocrisy" and "opportunistic behavior" in Golkar's Bambang Soesatyo and the PDI-P's Maruarar Sirait, legislators who had strongly supported the Bank Century bailout, but now sat on the committee of inquiry, denigrating Sri Mulyani through "media attacks." In the political environment of a new democracy, Yudhoyono remained more focused on restoring accommodations between parties than promoting reforms, leading to his "bewildering failure to defend his most senior colleagues and ministers from the outset" (*The Economist* 2010).

It was only after Yudhoyono finally voiced support for Sri Mulyani and Boediono that the "bailout farce" (*Asia Sentinel* 2010a) was finally settled. In what appears to have been a compromise, the DPR's inquiry committee declared the funding to have been illegal, but issued only a nonbinding ruling in favor of investigation. Boediono was left in place as vice-president. But legislators continued to hector Sri Mulyani in the Assembly or boycott sessions outright, finally prompting her to resign as finance minister and take up a directorship with the World Bank. In an interview, she attributed her decision directly to party leaders, legislators, and their business allies who resisted her reforms: "This time it's [Bakrie]....But I'm not denying there aren't others" (*Financial Times* 2010). Just two days after Sri Mulyani's departure, at a closed meeting of government parties held at Yudhoyono's home, a new joint secretariat was set up, which was described as "likely to play an important role in determining government policy" (*Asia Sentinel* 2010b). Aburizal Bakrie was appointed chairman, encouraging speculation that he sought to succeed Yudhoyono as president.

Thus, the ideological preferences that had once charged debate in the DPR over new electoral laws and constitutional amendments, distinguishing parties as "status quo" or "pro-democratic," have long evaporated. "Today, this cleavage is hardly reflected in the parliament at all," writes Andreas Ufen (2006: 10–11). As ideologies waned and procedures grew settled, legislators more single-mindedly pursued the patronage now available to them in abundance.

> *Once the fervor of democratization died down, DPR legislators turned their attention to patronage*

Though access to public resources has remained greatest at the cabinet level, rich stores of largesse have been extended to the DPR, deeply coloring the motivations of those who seek membership.

It is not simply that ideological preferences have been leveled across party vehicles. Although a feverish quest of patronage prevails, party leaders have moderated competition on even this count by perpetuating their legacies of networking and sharing resources in rough proportion to the number of DPR seats they hold. In the absence of an ideological foundation, or even sustained friction over the practice of largesse, little distinction appears between the government and the opposition. Accordingly, a lack of sharp-edged partisanship ensures that little meaningful horizontal accountability is imposed (Schneier 2004: 31). The legislature's powers of oversight offer, instead, the wherewithal to extort.

It is within the DPR's framework of commissions and committees that these activities most pulsate, with legislators meeting directly with ministers and other officials in hearings. Under the DPR's Rules of Procedure, all parties must be represented in each of the commissions. To ensure that parties have enough members to achieve this, they must reconfigure as caucuses (*fraksi*). Large secular parties such as Golkar, the PDI-P, and, after 2008, the Democrat Party have enough members in the DPR to each compose their own caucus. Smaller parties, though, often Islamic in hue, must band together to reach the minimal requirement of eleven members. In the proceedings that follow, the heads of commissions hold sway, with caucus leaders and members seldom dissenting.

The dynamics of the party cartel filter into the commissions and committees, with party leaders, through their networks, negotiating leadership and membership positions (Schneier 2004: 26). However, slippage has also grown evident, as members come to identify less with their party than with their commissions in everyday functioning (Mietzner and Aspinall 2010: 11). But even if refracted through commission settings, the norms of consensual decision making remain enforced by the Rules of Procedure. Deliberative sessions, then, while often open to the media and public, are typically short of spark and elocution. Stephen Sherlock (2007: 45) writes that members' speeches, only sketchily recorded, are "ill-prepared, un-researched, and 'off-the-cuff.'" In turn, their colleagues pay "little attention…and feel little compunction about wandering in and out of meetings." Further, in those instances where consensus remains elusive, commission heads and key members take to informal politics, conducting "closed lobbying" and "private meetings," frequently in the salons of Jakarta hotels. As no minutes are published, Sherlock (2007: 16) observes that the initial views of members can seldom be determined, nor can the methods by which dissenters are "persuaded" in these meetings to join in consensus.

> *Deliberations in commissions are typically "ill-prepared, un-researched, and 'off-the-cuff'"*

Amid this procedural opaqueness, members of commissions impose little horizontal accountability. Instead, they act on a greater motivation, using their powers of oversight to leverage patronage. Numerous analysts (e.g., Slater 2004, Schneier 2004, Pelizzo and Ang 2008) have recorded the corrupt practices that mar the DPR's functioning. Sherlock (2007: 39) writes bluntly of a "culture" in the assembly whereby members "treat the passage of a Bill not as a duty performed but as a favor which they should expect special recompense." Ordinary citizens lament, in turn, that "all our legislators know how to do is fight over their perks—houses, subsidies, cash" (Emmerson 2004: 95).

These exchanges turn most vitally on payments made by executive agencies or business firms to the heads of the DPR's commissions or subcommissions, in return for which they gain approvals for sundry legislative initiatives, regulatory actions, and government contracts. Payments percolate downward from the heads to ordinary members, showering them with patronage. Commissions are not equally lucrative, however, for some operate in policy areas that are regarded as "wetter," than others. Those with authority over state-owned enterprises, natural resources, transport, forestry, education, and health are especially "notorious for the exploitation for illegal income" (Sherlock 2007: 23). But even the members of the religious affairs commission are able to extract public resources, "skim[ming] the interest" from the deposits made by those who are preparing to make the pilgrimage to Mecca (Slater 2004: 67). As the exchanges between agencies and their partner commissions grow routinized, they solidify in symbiotic but distortive "sub-governments" (Schneier 2004: 26).

> *Even the religious affairs commission has skimmed resources from savings accounts for pilgrimages*

Patrick Ziegenhain provides numerous vignettes of the corruption that pervades the DPR, irrespective of party affiliations. He quotes a PDI-P member of the forestry commission who, in an interview in 2001 with the *Jakarta Post*, revealed that payments had been made by the Ministry of Forestry and Agriculture: "We convened for deliberation on the [plantation] bill for days and nights. It is normal for me to accept cash" (*Jakarta Post Online*, September 21, 2001, quoted in Ziegenhain 2008: 118). A member of the Star and Crescent Party (PBB) observed that bribery was "common practice" in various commissions, especially Commissions III, IV, V, VIII, and IX, whose responsibilities include banking and state enterprises (Ziegenhain 2008: 118). Two other PDI-P members of Commission IX disclosed that they were offered bribes by the country's asset management agency in order to gain approval for a bank sale. Other committee members, however, "kept silent or even criticized the whistle blowers" (ibid: 119–20). Another legislator labeled these practices as "envelope politics" and, though acknowledging them as corrupt, observed that "every faction was involved." Debates over the budget were described as especially lengthy because "the more legislators talked, the more money they could get from private and state-owned enterprises" (ibid: 71).

Sherlock (2007: 46) contends, however, that the most "egregious forms" of corruption have recently been curtailed through new requirements that legislators declare their assets, more rigorous controls on state-owned enterprises, closer scrutiny by the media and nongovernmental organizations (NGOs), and the unanticipated vigilance of the Corruption Eradication Commission (KPK) and the Anti-Corruption Court. But the regularity with which penalties have been imposed indicates the seriousness of corrupt practices and the extent to which they persist. In

> *Some of the most rampant forms of corruption among DPR members have recently been curtailed*

2007, for example, the Supreme Audit Agency (BPK) discovered that four years earlier, Bank Indonesia officials had made payments of some 31.5 billion rupiah to the heads of two subcommissions within the Finance and Banking Commission, both from Golkar. These heads had then distributed the money to the commission's chairman and its members. Convicted by the Anti-Corruption Court, they were sentenced to three and five years imprisonment (Irawaty 2009). In March 2009, two members of the Transport Commission, one from the National Mandate Party (PAN) and the other from the Reform Star Party, were convicted of taking payments for issuing government contracts, both garnering lengthy sentences (*Jakarta Globe* 2009). Legislators from the moderately Islamist National Awakening Party (PKB), as well as the PPP, have also been convicted. Indeed, since gaining cabinet-level positions, "prominent figures" within the Prosperous Justice Party (PKS), once firmly committed to the adoption of *shari'a* law, have been implicated in corruption scandals, amply illustrating Edward Aspinall's (2010: 29) thesis that most of Indonesia's Islamists "are more interested in sharing in the fruits of power than overthrowing it." Members of Yudhoyono's own Democrat Party have been jailed. More recently, "dozens of PDI-P politicians," though their leader stands in opposition to Yudhoyono, have been alleged by the Corruption Eradication Commission (KPK) to have taken "traveler cheques sealed in a brown envelope" in payment for arranging the approval in Commission X of the Central Bank's senior deputy governor in 2004 (*Jakarta Post* 2010).

In 2009, the DPR, in a rare display of legislative initiative, sought to protect its conduits to patronage by altering the statutes upon which the Corruption Eradication Commission (KPK) was based. Briefly, the agency had released wiretaps that implicated high-level police officials in bribing DPR members, as well as pressuring for the release of Bank Century funds to "well-paying entrepreneurs" (von Luebke 2010: 86).

As tensions mounted, the police likened the KPK's challenge to a "gecko versus a crocodile," and retaliated by arresting two KPK deputy directors on "vaguely defined charges." This triggered such mass-level protests that the officials were

The effectiveness of the Corruption Eradication Commission prompted the DPR to dilute its power

freed and reinstated by President Yudhoyono. Although this "frame-up" by police ultimately failed, the DPR proposed legislation in September 2009 that sought to strip the KPK of its powers to wiretap and prosecute. In the face of additional protests, the assembly eventually relented. But it then "diluted" the Corrupt Crimes Court in which the commission prosecutes its cases by requiring that its Jakarta-based unit, which had a 100 percent conviction rate, be replaced by smaller panels in all 33 of the country's provinces, the members of which would be selected by the Supreme Court (*Wall Street Journal,* 2009). In this way, the corruption court would be weakened, with "ad hoc judges," who were generally regarded as "reform-minded," superseded by old-style "career judges." Thus, the DPR used its legislative powers, as it did its powers of oversight, to protect its patronage rather than to promote good governance and horizontal accountability.

Low Accountability in the Philippines

As in Indonesia since 2004, presidents in the Philippines earn legitimation through direct election, which diminishes their need for gaining it through congressional oversight. At the same time, legislators are usually uninterested in imposing oversight. Even when President Joseph Estrada's corruption and policy ineptness drove the House of Representatives to impeach him, his allies in the Senate lent him cover. Estrada's ouster was never finalized by Congress but, instead, by the resumption of street protests, labeled People Power II, and by the sanction given by the military and Supreme Court. Further, Estrada's successor and his vice-president, Gloria Macapagal-Arroyo, sought to avoid his fate by greatly accelerating patronage flows, precipitating what Nathan Quimpo (2009) describes as a qualitative shift on the political scene from "old-style patronage politics" to "brazen predatory politics." Hence, in effectively sating the lower house, Arroyo finished out Estrada's term and, after winning election in 2004, completed her own, securing her status as the country's longest-serving president, save Marcos.

> *Gloria Macapagal-Arroyo sought to avoid Estrada's fate by accelerating already substantial patronage flows*

In its institutional framework and procedures, Congress is highly elaborated and formalized. Even more than Indonesia's DPR, Congress thus possesses seemingly powerful mechanisms by which to check the executive. Nearly 60 committees in the House of Representatives are each tasked with overseeing a related bureaucratic entity. There are also four that are dedicated solely to accountability functions. The Committee on Oversight, with 21–25 members, was set up during the 14th Congress to address major cases of corruption. The Committee on Good Government examines more ordinary cases involving corrupt practices. The Committee on Ethics passes judgment on the alleged misbehaviors of the representatives themselves. And the large Committee on Justice, with 55 members, evaluates the merit of impeachment complaints that have been lodged in the House. One such complaint is permitted each year. If the committee, after holding hearings, finds the complaint "sufficient in substance," and gains the support of just one-third of the representatives in a plenary vote, it is forwarded to the Senate for an impeachment trial.

In performing oversight, these lower house committees are supported by permanent secretariats that include trained lawyers. High-level investigations in the Senate, carried out by the Blue Ribbon Committee, are supported by the Blue Ribbon Oversight Office Management (BROOM). Committees in both houses are empowered to subpoena executive officials. Their sessions are usually open to the public. Recommendations to bring charges are then forwarded to the Office of the Ombudsman, which determines whether prosecution is warranted in the *Sandiganbayan*, the country's corruption court.

But in interviews conducted in mid-2010 at the House of Representatives complex in Quezon City, committee staff members complained repeatedly of shortcomings in accountability. Though they themselves might diligently carry out the investigations that are ordered, the reports that they produce, though exhaustive and duly posted on the government's website, typically languish in committee, then finally are "archived." Thus, the chief legal officer for a deputy House Speaker (interview 2010), in commenting on oversight, reflected that "in reality, very little of this takes place." Committees usually meet twice a month, but their power to subpoena executive officials for hearings is "never exercised vigorously." Even when they appear, "officials [are] generally uncooperative." Further, only lesser bureaucrats can now be summoned, after Arroyo imposed a controversial measure in 2006, Executive Order 464, barring department secretaries and undersecretaries from hearings without the president's approval. Committees are also bound by a Supreme Court ruling handed down late in her tenure that all investigations be conducted "in aid of legislation," ostensibly to prevent the "fishing expeditions" that erode a constitutionally mandated separation of powers. In an interview (2010), a newly elected senator referred derisively to this requirement as "a joke. No legislation ever comes out of investigation." Thus, the executive has been given yet another tool with which to avoid accountability.

In its operation, then, the Committee on Oversight, "has done little" (representative staff legal officer interview 2010). The permanent staff members of the Committee on Good Government, which were handed 60 complaints during the 14th Congress, sometimes conveyed by representatives through what is labeled a "privilege speech," but more often through anonymous letters, referred only one case back to the committee recommending prosecution (Good Government Committee staff member interview 2010). The Ethics Committee has been even less active. In responding to sworn complaints during the 14th Congress, the Committee wrote two reports, one of which was "withdrawn" and the second "set aside" (Ethics Committee staff member interview 2010). Thus, while bureaucrats are occasionally prosecuted for corrupt practices, no staff member interviewed could recall a congressman having ever been similarly charged, much less removed from office. In consequence, a high-level Liberal Party official (interview 2010) lamented that with oversight so weak, "syndicates [operate unchecked] in Immigration, Customs, Education, the courts, everywhere."

> *The lackluster Committee on Good Government recommended prosecution in only one case*

Nor has any president ever been ousted through the impeachment process, whatever their seeming misdeeds. In interviews, representatives and staff members repeatedly characterized impeachment as a "numbers game," its dynamics highly partisan, rather than any serious exercise in accountability. Usually, complaints have been lodged by a single representative and supported by a small group. They are then referred to the Justice Committee, which in all cases except the one involving Estrada has recommended that it be dismissed as groundless. Although the committee's report and accompanying resolution must next be sent to the House, representatives usually vote in large margins to support its judgment. The action taken against Estrada was thus unique, attributable to his failing to control the House in the way that Arroyo had. When asked why in an interview (2010), a legal officer of a leading representative explained, "because he was not so scheming."

During the long tenure of Arroyo, four impeachment complaints were filed against her. The first, mounted in 2005, involved allegations of her colluding with the electoral commission (COMELEC) to cheat in the previous year's contest, hence "robbing the sovereign will" (Committee on Justice 2005: 27). But despite the outcry that followed, fueled by the infamous "Hello, Garci" audio recording (see

GMA News Research 2008), a resolution to dismiss the complaint was accepted on the floor by a vote of 158–52. With even greater ease, Arroyo would parry the next three impeachment complaints—one introduced every year, just as the constitution permits.

Even so, it is instructive to examine the final impeachment complaint, filed in 2008, for it shows that while executive abuses in new democracies may grow extensive, accountability can largely be avoided. In April 2007, the president's office announced that the government had signed an agreement in China with ZTE, a Chinese telecommunications firm, to set up a national broadband network (NBN) for $329.5 million that would link Philippine government offices across the country (see GMA NewsTV 2009b). The NBN-ZTE deal was vastly more expensive than other bids that had been submitted—one for $240 million from Amsterdam Holdings, owned by Joey de Venecia III, son of House Speaker Jose de Venecia; and another for $135 million from Arescom, a US company (Bordadora and Dizon 2007). In August, a representative alleged in a privilege speech that the chairman of the Commission on Elections, Benjamin Abalos, had met with ZTE officials to broker the deal. Later, while asking for some $130 million in commissions from ZTE, Abalos was alleged to have offered payment to the secretary of the National Economic Planning Authority (NEDA), Romulo Neri, to approve the deal.

Joey de Venecia then claimed publicly that the contract had been corruptly awarded. In September, the Senate Committee on Accountability of Public Officers and Investigations, less formally titled the Blue Ribbon Committee, responded by opening an investigation. It subpoenaed de Venecia, who then testified that President Arroyo's husband "Mike" had pushed vigorously for the project. He stated that he had been warned to "back off" in his own bid by the "first gentleman." Amid public fury, President Arroyo suspended the contract. But de Venecia continued to testify to the Senate, alleging in October that of the $130 million that Abalos had demanded, $70 million was to have been passed on to Mike Arroyo.

Meanwhile, BROOM's lawyers investigated closely. Asked during interviews (2010) to estimate the scale of corruption under Arroyo, one of them replied, "On a scale of 0–10? 8.75. [Corruption was] pervasive." He depicted the abuses in the NBN-ZTE case as "blatant." He characterized the $70 million that the president's husband had allegedly sought as equal to the "combined budgets of two or three small provinces." He described Joey de Venecia as "disgruntled, so [he] squealed,"

> *The 'president was unable to control her own men as they fought over their kickbacks'*

while "the executive stonewalled." Upon completing its investigation, made difficult by the case's technical and diplomatic aspects, as well as the Supreme Court's in-aid-of-legislation ruling that was issued "at the height of the ZTE controversy," BROOM (Committee on Accountability of Public Officers and Investigations 2009: 1) forwarded a substantive report to the Blue Ribbon Committee. It stated bluntly:

> In the middle of it all is a president who was unable to control and discipline her own men as they fight over their kickbacks....If people look at the opportunists in this scandal, they will discover that they are all scavengers and predators....And when they cannot get their rightful share of the booty, one of them squeals and they start pointing fingers at another.

Meanwhile, with Jose de Venecia's son having testified before the Senate, pressure mounted for his ouster as speaker in the House of Representatives. De Venecia had long been helpful to Arroyo, even supporting her calls for the abolition of the Senate and adoption of a parliamentary system, presumably so that she might avoid the term limit that presidents faced. But now, de Venecia's party, Lakas, after caucusing in October, recommended that he "go quietly" by resigning. After he refused, he was ousted by the representatives in February 2008 through a motion of no confidence. He was succeeded by Prospero Nograles, portrayed as "a close ally of Arroyo" (Conde 2008).

In the same month, the Office of the Ombudsman started its own investigation into the NBN-ZTE case. A year-and-a-half later, it reported that President Arroyo enjoyed immunity from any charges while in office, then cleared her husband, the secretary of Transport and Communications, and other officials who had been implicated. It only recommended that charges be brought against Abalos and Neri, the secretary of NEDA. For ruling in so partisan a way, the ombudsman, frequently portrayed in the media as "an old classmate" of Mike Arroyo, was herself impeached. But by effectively preempting the Senate, the Blue Ribbon Committee's proceedings were quickly wound down.

Jose de Venecia, his son, and others responded by filing an impeachment complaint against Arroyo in the House of Representatives for "betrayal of public trust…through her involvement in the NBN-ZTE deal" (Committee on Justice 2008: 2). They also cited other "high crimes," including the "Hello, Garci" case. Days later, the Department of Justice retaliated by releasing its findings that the bid made by Amsterdam Holdings for the broadband project had constituted improper influence and a conflict of interest. No mention was made of President Arroyo or her husband. After concluding its hearings, the Justice Committee, chaired by yet another of the president's allies, Matias Defensor, dismissed the impeachment complaint by a vote of 42 to 8. Stating that its "recycled and rehashed grounds [had] been previously adjudicated and dismissed in the prior impeachment cases" (Committee on Justice 2008: 16), the complaint was found to be insufficient in substance. Sent to a plenary session, the committee's resolution and report were adopted by a vote of 183 to 21.

How had President Arroyo come to so thoroughly dominate the House of Representatives? To be sure, she faced staunch ideological resistance from some party list members, a cohort introduced in 1998 and given 20 percent of the House's seats in order to represent historically marginalized groups, such as teachers, migrant workers, women, and Muslim communities. Representatives from progressive parties and coalitions like Akbayan and Bayan Muna strongly criticized the government's record on social issues. However, unlike proportional representation systems used elsewhere, the version deployed in the Philippines capped the number of seats that any one party could win at three, exacerbating the organizational dispersion common in such systems. At the same time, with many parties failing to win one-fiftieth of the total votes cast, which is required to gain entry to the House, some party list seats are left unfilled (Boudreau 2010: 110). What is more, during Arroyo's presidency, the party list system came to be used as a "back door" for candidates with whom she was allied. These included her wealthy son "Mikey," who had won nomination for the 2010 election from a sector organization that incorporated low-paid security guards, jeepney and tricycle drivers, and street vendors. Arroyo's sister-in-law also won nomination for a party list seat, as did a former army general whom she favored, Jovito Palparan, who has been blamed for many extrajudicial killings of activists and journalists. In explanation, the chairman of COMELEC pleaded in 2010 that the commission was quite unable to "screen" party list nominees (Tan 2010).

Arroyo gained an even tighter grip on district-based representatives. Presidents in the Philippines, far more than their counterparts in Indonesia, have kept control over patronage flows. Most representatives, keenly aware that their speechmaking and voting records in the House matter less for their reelection to office than procuring funding for their districts, have been dissuaded from testing the executive by imposing accountability. Thus, while the budget is reviewed by Congress, it is distorted by a "high degree of executive prerogative" (Hutchcroft 2007). Specifically, the legislature is permitted to reduce the budget items

> *Speechmaking and voting records are far less significant for reelection than pork'*

that the president proposes, but it cannot increase them. Further, only the president can release the funds once they have been appropriated. While Arroyo was in power, she went further by introducing a "conditional vet," which permitted her to impound funds that had been included by Congress in general appropriations acts and shift them to special purpose funds "under the control of the president [and] out of reach of Congress" (Social Watch Philippines 2009).

In addition, the president controls the Priority Development Assistance Fund (PDAF), introduced in 2000 under Estrada as a successor program to the Country Development Fund. Through the PDAF, 70 million pesos may be allocated annually to each sitting representative (and 200 million pesos to each senator). Widely derided as pork, the PDAF is also essential to representatives who seek to energize loyalties in their districts. Half of their disbursements involve small public work projects that representatives select. Less than a fifth is committed to education, health, water supply, and other vital services (House of Representatives, n.d.). Still, top politicians vigorously defend its use. A House Speaker in the 14th Congress, Prospero Nograles, and the chairman of the appropriations committee, Edcel Lagman (Nograles and Lagman n.d.: 12), authored an extraordinary document in which they defend discretionary expenditures made under the PDAF as bringing "government closer to the people" in ways that are socially beneficial, quite unlike the "sinful 'pork barrel' of the original American mould." More colorfully, President Arroyo, after opening the Ozamiz Airport in the Visayas in 2007 that had been "bankrolled" by Congress, exclaimed, "Now, that's the kind of pork that has good cholesterol" (Ubac 2007).

Although formal reporting mechanisms are in place, a long-time representative's chief of staff disclosed in an interview (2010) that it was "SOP" (standard operating procedure) for representatives to take "commissions" when distributing contracts. In this way, they held some funds in reserve that could be allocated more tactically, either to shore up the sagging allegiances of local officials in their districts or to line their own pockets. Even more brashly, representatives have steered contracts directly to their own companies or those operated by relatives and in-laws (Ilagan 2009). Accordingly, on the congressional website, most projects involve road and pathway "concretization" and "rehabilitation of drains," or, more nebulously, the construction of "multipurpose buildings" and "multipurpose pavements" (House of Representatives n.d.).

> *Projects for 'concretization,' 'rehabilitation of drains,' and 'multipurpose pavements' are steered by legislators to their own companies*

Some legislators have complained that Arroyo usurped from Congress "the power of the purse." Indeed, she withheld appropriations, as well as vital PDAF payments, from representatives who defied her. She also continued a long-standing practice of holding up revenue allocations, granted under the Local Government Code, to "uncooperative" provincial and local officials (Abinales 2008: 297–98). For those who remained loyal, however, Arroyo released funding in great volume. She was also alleged to have made direct payments to representatives, especially in preparation for votes on impeachment (just as many representatives had planned, thus encouraging them now to retreat from the impeachment complaints that they had earlier mounted [interview, representative's chief of staff, 2010]).

At the same time, Arroyo nurtured the clan lineages in which most representatives are rooted, freely releasing revenues to governors, provincial board members, mayors, and councilors. They, in turn, delivered votes for her and the legislators with whom she was allied. She also forged fresh links with traditional Muslim clans in the Autonomous Region of Muslim Mindanao (ARMM), an area char-

Arroyo nurtured the clan lineages in which most Congressmen are rooted

acterized by a former official in the Department of Education as a "black hole" (interview 2010). It was in this way that the notorious Ampatuan family secured its stronghold in Maguindanao and attracted funding by creating ever more municipalities (Hutchcroft 2008: 150).

Through such measures, Arroyo won the "unwavering and wholehearted support" of the country's governors, who joined forces in the influential League of Provinces of the Philippines (League of Provinces of the Philippines 2008).

In this context, shortly after ascending to the presidency, Arroyo, like executives before her, gained overwhelming support in the House of Representatives. In voting for her choice for Speaker, Jose de Venecia, representatives signaled their wish to join the House majority. They then sealed their new loyalties by flocking to her party or ruling coalition. Thus, by swelling their ranks with "immigrants," as they are locally termed, "the president's party is the majority party" (Liberal Party official interview 2010).

Arroyo, thus, tightened her "hold on the House" when her party vehicle KAMPI (Partner of the Free Filipino) coalesced with Lakas and the Christian and Muslim Democrats (CMD) to form the Lakas-CMD-KAMPI coalition. Her candidacy also drew the support of the Liberal Party and, later, of the Nationalist People's Coalition (NPC), a group that had broken from the Nacionalistas during the early 1990s. After her election in 2004, she controlled 191 of the 221 seats in the House of Representatives. Only in 2006, after release of the Garci tapes encouraged a faction of Liberal Party members to leave the majority, hence splitting the party, did the House minority gain any standing.

At the start of each new Congress, the Speaker takes recommendations from the majority and minority leaders and assigns committee chairmanships and memberships that, like the commissions in Indonesia's DPR, open more avenues to substantive patronage. The House currently has 58 departmental committees and 12 "special" committees

(GMA NewsTV 2009a). But they bear different levels of largesse, with Appropriations, Rules, Ways and Means, Appointments, Banking, Public Works, Transportation, Agriculture, Fisheries, and Games and Amusement the most prized. Although falling shy of the level of accommodation that prevails in Indonesia's DPR, Jose de Venecia awarded positions broadly enough across the majority's parties and factions that "rainbow coalitions" were created (Philippines Center for Independent Journalism, hereafter PCIJ, 2004a). In the 14th Congress, the Appropriations Committee grew to include 125 members, nearly half the legislature's membership of 268. As these committees proceeded to grant approvals for state contracts, licenses, and franchises, they extracted payments from beneficiaries in the bureaucracy and business (PCIJ 2004b).

By contrast, the Senate claims that its nationwide constituency reduces its need for pork, leaving it better poised to check the executive. Indeed, Senator Franklin Drilon (interview 2010) stated, "We get PDAF, but we don't need it [to win reelection]." Further, he asserts, "because Congress is—I don't want to say subservient, but *supportive* of the president—this is why we need a Senate." Though Drilon backed Arroyo at the time of her election in 2004, he turned sharply against her the following year over her allegedly influencing COMELEC. It was also the Senate's comparative autonomy that enabled it to investigate the NBN-ZTE case so thoroughly. However, as we have seen, by controlling the Ombudsman and other executive agencies, President Arroyo was finally able to ward off the accountability that the Senate tried to impose.

But more than this, the Senate has suffered from intrinsic deficiencies in its institutional functioning. Though some senators may eschew pork, others still build national followings by "cut[ting their] own deals with local power holders throughout the archipelago" (Hutchcroft 2008: 153). For example, in the 2007 election, some 30 million pesos were paid by "a northern Luzon strongman...for the top

> *Senators amass national followings by cutting deals with local power holders throughout the archipelago*

senatorial slot" in the far-off province of Maguindanao (ibid: 150). Moreover, after having secured their vast constituencies, senators often acquire commensurately large ambitions. In an interview (2010), a newly elected senator insisted that the upper house "can get things done." But because many of his new colleagues were "presidents-in-waiting," the Senate was given to "grandstanding" and often "distracted by political theater." When asked about the frequent criticism that the upper house is deliberately "obstructionist" in its dealings with the president and the representatives, the senator conceded that "there is some truth in this."

At the same time, with most representatives geared tightly to what is characterized as "constituency work," the interest in serious legislation and debate remains scant. Thus, the "quiet ones" in the House vastly outnumber the "vocal ones" (interview, representative's chief of staff 2010). The minority leader in the 15th Congress, Edcel Lagman, conceded that "there is not much deliberation on the bills. That is why what is harnessed as a final version might be defective or of interior quality." The representative for the 1st District of Bukidnon, Nereus Acosta Jr., noted similarly that "deliberations are bereft of policy discussions" (Ordenes-Cascolan 2007). In an interview (2010), Senator Ferdinand Marcos Jr. contended that in Congress proposing bills has become a popular "test" of legislative activity, encouraging "filing and filing and filing." Few bills, however, become law. By the end of the second year of 14th Congress, 7,791 measures had been filed by members, but only 147 were enacted (House of Representatives 2009: 2). Further, the bulk of these laws were "local" rather than national in their content, generally involving the establishment or reorganization of schools and the naming and renaming of roads and bridges.

> *Of the 7,791 measures that were filed in the 14th Congress, only 147 laws were enacted, most for reorganizing schools or renaming roads and bridges*

Much needed legislation, then, such as the Anti–Political Dynasty Bill, which was intended to operationalize provisions in the 1987 Constitution, and the Freedom of Access to Information Act, first introduced in 1992, languish in the committees to which they were referred. Outside "pressure groups" are sometimes to blame, such as the Responsible Parenthood and Populations Management Act, first presented in 1985, which was strongly opposed by the Catholic Church, or the Human

Rights Compensation Bill, which has been held up by the military (representative's legal officer, interview, 2010). But even when bills are passed by the House, they may bog down in Senate proceedings. As Jose de Venecia (2007: 1) wrote before being deposed as Speaker, "tragically, 966 House measures were stranded in the Senate—a spectacle that dramatizes the wastage of our time, efforts, and resources."

In sum, with representatives strongly prioritizing patronage, therein negating their motivations to impose accountability or undertake legislation, President Arroyo found the lower house quite manageable. She thwarted their weak efforts to unseat her, then, despite "revelation after revelation" of corrupt dealings involving her family members and political allies (Abinales 2008: 299). Put simply, by shrewdly widening the cornucopia of corruption, she avoided accountability for her corruption. Only in mid-2010, then, with her presidency finished and her control over patronage ended did Arroyo's party coalition dissolve and punishment loom. But by then, the damage to democracy in the Philippines had been done. As mentioned above, the regime's status was downgraded by Freedom House in 2006 from "free" to "partly free."

Greater Accountability in Malaysia
If in Indonesia and the Philippines legislatures have misused their powers to impose horizontal accountability, their counterpart in Malaysia has sometimes applied its power, though more modest, with positive effect. With Malaysia's politics having settled into electoral authoritarianism, the opposition has been galvanized by the nested two-tier game in which it is engaged, striving to ignite democratic transition, while tirelessly criticizing the government's everyday policymaking.

> *Executives in Malaysia boost their legitimation by tolerating the limited accountability that the opposition imposes*

At the same time, in seeking to more efficiently obtain compliance from citizens, the executive has boosted the legitimation of electoral authoritarian rule by tolerating the limited accountability that the opposition imposes. Unlike Indonesia's presidents, then, who have resisted any interpellation by the DPR, Malaysia's prime ministers appear in Parliament periodically, personally introducing budgets and major

William Case

legislative initiatives. And at least a few cabinet ministers, deputy ministers, or parliamentary secretaries are also in attendance during routine question time.

Historically, opposition has been spearheaded by the DAP. Publicly committed to democratization, good governance, and mild socialist redistribution, but more popularly associated with ethnic Chinese grievances over the NEP, the party has usually held 10–20 seats in the legislature, most of them representing urban Chinese districts. PAS has also been publicly committed to electoral fairness and good governance, though suspicions persist among secular middle-class Malays and the Chinese that the party secretly prioritizes the adoption of *shari'a* law. Accordingly, PAS has usually held fewer seats than the DAP, though it did lead the opposition for a term after registering strong gains in the 1999 election. Finally, with many middle-class Malays unable to abide Barisan, the DAP, or PAS, they have turned to the People's Justice Party (PKR), which traces its lineage to the jailing of a former deputy prime minster, Anwar Ibrahim, a decade ago. In Malaysia's most recent election held in March 2008, the PKR mediated relations between the DAP and PAS, then led an informal coalition that won 81 parliamentary seats, therein denying Barisan its customary two-thirds majority. Thus, in having maintained discipline across parties, while articulating reasonably coherent ideological commitments against electoral unfairness, corrupt practices, and the inequities of the NEP, vertical accountability was bolstered. Anwar assumed the role of opposition leader in Parliament, though remained thwarted in his drive to form a new government.

However, if the opposition has failed under electoral authoritarianism to gain power, an outcome that would amount to "democratization-by-election," what mechanisms has it used to try to hold the executive accountable? As noted above, there is little prospect that the opposition will attract enough defectors to successfully mount a no-confidence vote. Nor can it summon and monitor executive officials through any meaningful system of committees shadowing corresponding departments, the absence of which appears to be a legacy of British colonial governance (Barkan 2009: 10). While select committees do exist formally, they have historically been convened only rarely and their role has remained advisory. Five "sessional" committees also exist and are more regularly summoned, but are geared mostly to "housekeeping" matters. Thus, only the

Public Accounts Committee (PAC), whose task is to determine whether the budget has been properly disbursed, performs any serious oversight role. But it remains, like all other committees, chaired by a government legislator. And it is dependent on the auditor-general's report for even such limited information as it obtains.

Thus, Noore Alam Siddiquee (2006: 47, 49) records that because committees are "toothless," debates, parliamentary questions, supplementary questions, and motions offer the only "devices" by which the legislature can impose accountability. He also contends that notwithstanding the limited scope that these avenues permit, the government's Barisan members of parliament (MPs) rarely exploit them, for fear that any deviation from the "party line" will "jeopardize their ambitions" for party nominations and ministerial positions (Noore 2006: 49).

It falls squarely to opposition legislators to impose horizontal accountability. To this end, they regularly propose different kinds of motions (Fuzi Omar 2008: 34–37), but only one-third are entertained by the speaker as sufficiently "urgent," "specific," and "of interest to the public" to be recognized. Even when debates do take place, they are frequently cut off because not enough government legislators are in attendance to meet quorum (Noore 2006: 49). In those cases where voting takes place, it is always won overwhelmingly by Barisan. With respect to question time, "the most important proceeding in Parliament" (Fuzi Omar 2008: 38), though ministers, deputy ministers, or parliamentary secretaries might appear, legislators in opposition face hurdles in using these encounters effectively. Questions must be submitted in writing several weeks in advance of each of the three sessions that Parliament convenes each year. Thus, the answers that are finally given by ministers or their deputies are generally stale (DAP legislator interview, 2008). Although several dozen questions are typically accepted, question time is kept to an hour, preventing queries near the end of the list from ever being addressed.

Opposition legislators are hampered also by a lack of legislative resources. Though government ministers come armed with responses that have been ably prepared by civil servants, opposition legislators are prevented from similarly sourcing information by the Official Secrets Act. The Parliamentary Research Unit provides no adequate substitute, as its ten staff members are only able to perform "minimal tasks" (ibid.). Members are given no funding with which to hire their own staff or to open a parliamentary office. And they are distracted from "policy development" by the frequent need to perform "constituency surgeries" and continuous "casework," lest they risk electoral defeat. Indeed, one PAS legislator (interview 2008) representing a rural constituency in the northern "Malay heartland" reported that voters often approached him for personal loans, which, when reluctantly granted, seemed to encourage additional requests. In this context, a DAP legislator (interview 2008) flatly characterized the role of an opposition parliamentarian as a "bloody frustrating experience."

One DAP legislator described the role of opposition parliamentarian as a 'bloody frustrating experience'

Even so, in seeking simultaneously to increase political space and to modify public policy, many opposition members have sought steadfastly to impose accountability. In a content analysis of parliamentary debates during Tun Mahathir bin Mohamad's long tenure as prime minister from 1981–2003, Muhamad Fuzi Omar (2008) identifies the kinds of issues that the opposition has regularly raised and instances in which the government has sometimes obliged it. As noted above, few of the motions proposed by the opposition have been accepted by the Speaker. But in entering the debates that are launched by the government's introducing its own motions at will, DAP legislators have seized opportunities to criticize the government over authoritarian controls, policy ineffectiveness, and corrupt practices, many of which are associated with the opaque privatization of state assets and police abuses. PAS legislators have also denounced the government over corruption, the detention of students and activists, and insufficient attention to Islam.

Fuzi Omar (2008: 38) declares that opposition legislators have been able to make even better use of question time, generating "heated exchanges" between MPs, securing "direct verbal answers" from ministers, and sometimes extracting policy concessions. He notes (2008: 38-41) that at different junctures in Mahathir's prime ministership, DAP legislators won guarantees from ministers over continued support for Chinese-language education in primary and secondary schools, changes from pro-Malay quotas to merit-based selection for university enrollment, an amendment to the Education Act to allow the formation of private universities, and greater permissiveness over ethnic festivals and cultural celebrations. In addition, PAS members gained greater government funding for religious schools, as well as revisions in cultural policies. The government agreed to changes in police uniform codes, for example, in order to allow female officers to wear the *hijab*.

More recently, in interviews conducted in late 2008, opposition legislators described the highly innovative ways by which their parties have strived to circumvent the institutional impediments that they face. Under a category of strategies labeled as "adversarial," the opposition makes clever use of supplementary questions, treating them as opportunities "where you can do something funny" (DAP legislator interview 2008). As one example, in responding during question time to a query that had been posed by a UMNO backbencher about the NEP, an official in the prime minister's department simply read out a lengthy answer. The DAP leader, Lim Kit Siang, feigning disbelief, intoned loudly that "the answer has been prepared." A PAS legislator chimed in, "the answer was so prepared that it runs to two pages." Having "caught the eye" of the chamber's startled Speaker, another DAP legislator was permitted to ask a second supplementary question about whether the minister even understood the principle of affirmative action. A fellow member of the opposition then interjected, "See whether he can answer the question now." This encouraged such jeering of the minister that the assembly's proceedings were described by an angry government legislator as having deteriorated into a "marketplace" (Beh, 2008a). Through such stratagems, Fuzi Omar suggests (2008: 41), "the negative responses notwithstanding, the opposition MPs contributed toward the process of check and balance of government activities through the answers provided to them."

Additional strategies intended to embarrass the government have included proposing parliamentary motions to cut the salaries of targeted ministers by an irksome "ten dollars," a process that under Standing Orders automatically triggers debate; heckling and booing in reaction to vexing statements made by government legislators, or loud "table-thumping" in support of fellow opposition members' sharp ripostes; and walkouts, usually mounted over perceptions of the Speaker's procedural unfairness. More substantively, the opposition has occasionally gained information that enables it to expose executive abuses in Parliament. Its findings are then publicized through press conferences which, even if ignored by mainstream outlets, are widely disseminated by new media, including blogs that—quite in contrast to technically less savvy legislators in Indonesia—are vigorously mounted by opposition members in Malaysia. Past instances of such revelations include the state-owned Bank Bumiputra's corrupt practices and large losses while trying to fulfill NEP quotas during the early 1980s; Mahathir's admission in Parliament during the late 1980s that UMNO had secured government contracts in order to finance its new headquarters; a gross misallocation of public money by the UMNO minister of tourism and culture in 2007; and the disclosure in 2008 that the inspector general of police had requested that the Finance Ministry approve the purchase of helicopters from a company associated with his son. These latter cases resulted in the government changing policy directions, with the tourism minister forced finally from office, while the helicopter deal was cancelled.

> *Executive abuses have been publicized by the opposition through press conferences and new media*

Under a category of "bipartisan" strategies, the opposition has sometimes sought to collaborate with amenable members of government, an approach that became more viable during the recent prime ministership of Abdullah Badawi. Recognizing that the UMNO-led government's legitimacy had faded toward the end of his predecessor Mahathir's tenure, Abdullah sought to bolster horizontal accountability (Case, 2010). The core dimensions of the electoral authoritarian regime remained unchanged, with most restrictions on civil liberties left in place. But Abdullah loosened controls on the legislature, enabling it to grow more active. And after the stunning election of March 2008, the opposition was better able to seize the moment, its ranks having swollen to more than a third of the Parliament's 222 seats.

In interviews, opposition legislators stated that in consequence, one accommodative UMNO parliamentarian, Shahrir Samad, chair of the Public Accounts Committee, had acted on a request from the DAP leader, Lim Kit Siang, to appoint a member of the opposition as the committee's deputy head. Thus, the PAC quickly enhanced its standing as nonpartisan and mildly effective, as it called witnesses and issued reports. In addition, more select committees were convened to scrutinize the government's legislative initiatives. Though still chaired by government MPs, those in opposition were able for the first time to affix amendments that were unpopular with government agencies. As one example, in 2008, the Select Committee for Criminal Procedural Code and Penal Code made changes to an existing remand law that, in softening the 14-day remand period to two seven-day segments, greatly antagonized the Attorney General's chambers.

During the final months of 2008, as his prime ministership waned, Abdullah personally tabled three bills in Parliament, the first of which sought to replace Malaysia's much discredited Anti-Corruption Agency with the new Malaysian Anti-Corruption Commission (MACC). Abdullah and the deputy prime minister, Najib Razak, then remained in Parliament for two days of "vigorous" debate (Beh 2008b), after which the opposition leader, Anwar Ibrahim, gave his "conditional backing." Lim Kit Siang "congratulated [the prime minister] for finally pushing for...a more powerful anti-corruption body." The bill passed, paving the way for the MACC's formation, regarded at the time as "an improved version over the present ACA" (Kim 2008).

A second bill, designed to increase the independence of the courts by creating a Judicial Accounts Commission (JAC), was found to be so skewed by even government legislators that they sided with the opposition in debate, then proposed some amendments (Beh 2008c). Hailing such new cooperation with government MPs, however rare, one PAS member (interview 2008) declared that "we bang the table for them now too." A final bill, intended to subject the police force to greater scrutiny by an Enforcement Agency Integrity Commission (EAIC), drew particular ire from opposition legislators. Indeed, in concert with human rights groups, the opposition raised so much public criticism that the bill was withdrawn, then reintroduced in a modified form after Abdullah's departure.

The dynamics that underlie these three legislative initiatives make plain that, in Malaysia, a motivated opposition has occasionally gone beyond merely checking the executive. Despite its limited parliamentary powers, it has been able to encourage

The opposition in Malaysia has imposed accountability in ways that are difficult to imagine in Indonesia

the government to alter legislation. Or, when it has viewed bills as too deeply flawed on procedural grounds, the opposition has in a few instances forced their withdrawal. Such outcomes remain difficult to imagine in Indonesia's DPR where, in the absence of coherent opposition, legislators have mostly been motivated to confront the executive in defense of their patronage.

However, after the opposition made gains in the 2008 election, enabling the Pakatan Rakyat to win control over four state governments while retaining a fifth, some of its officials appeared to engage in corrupt practices, hence illustrating our thesis in another way. As a tipping point in the transition from an old electoral authoritarian regime to a new democracy seemed to be reached, some state assemblymen and local councilors shifted their ambitions from advancing democratic change to pursuing patronage. In Selangor in late 2010, the Pakatan state government was revealed by the media to have been secretly investigating allegations that a third-term DAP municipal councilor had helped to secure contracts for "cronies and a family member." Indeed, Dzulkefly Ahmad (2010), a PAS MP, writes that "many of these small-time appointed councilors are causing much embarrassment to the Pakatan Rakyat coalition." It was reported also that some Pakatan officials in Selangor had issued "support letters" for friends to gain state contracts. At the same time, the Pakatan government, recalling its treatment while in opposition, began withholding constituency development funds from Barisan assemblymen in Selangor. Allegations were made also of illegal sand mining in Selangor and logging concessions that were corruptly awarded in Kelantan. In these circumstances, fears arose that the "PR will emulate BN-style patronage politics and practices now that they have tasted power" (Ding 2010).

Legislatures and Accountability in Cambodia and Singapore

Our best example of electoral authoritarianism in Southeast Asia remains Malaysia. For more than three decades, its government has limited civil liberties, while manipulating multiparty elections, keeping its politics on beam, at least until 2008. In this section, Cambodia and Singapore are briefly assessed. In both Southeast Asian countries, electoral authoritarian regimes persist, but civil liberties and electoral competitiveness have been more seriously truncated. These countries amount to hard cases, then, in which to scour for additional evidence that under conditions of electoral authoritarianism some legislators strive to impose accountability. With lines drawn firmly between the government and the opposition, most members of the opposition remain barred from joining the government and imbibing state patronage. They are motivated, then, to advance democratic transitions and policy changes, in the service of which they tirelessly expose executive abuses.

But equally, the cases of Cambodia and Singapore show why executives, in seeking to extend their tenure interminably, have stopped short of crushing the opposition's efforts. In Cambodia, with gross electoral manipulations dampening vertical accountability, the government has sought to compensate for the resulting deficits in legitimacy by tolerating, at least until recently, some opposition activities in its National Assembly. In Singapore, by contrast, though the government has also manipulated elections, its celebrated economic performance has plainly offset legitimacy deficits. Its re-

> *Even in 'hard' cases of electoral authoritarian rule in Cambodia and Singapore, executives stopped short of crushing the opposition*

fusal to admit many elected opposition members to Parliament, then, appears to have borne few costs. However, though it needs little legitimation, the government has introduced a surrogate opposition that, by mildly imposing some horizontal accountability, generates information. But the government has not sought to learn about the "true" levels of elite-level patronage cited by Boix and Svolik (n.d.). Rather, it has tried to gain insights into the preferences of new and illegible social forces.

Cambodia

Democratic change has remained stunted in Cambodia. It was "implanted" by external forces, namely, the United Nations Transitional Authority in Cambodia (UNTAC). And though UNTAC authored a democratic constitution and organized competitive elections in 1993, it found uncongenial soil in the country's low levels of economic development and opportunities for independent wealth creation. Severe impediments have also been posed by the outlooks of government leaders. As David Chandler (quoted in Johnston 2009a: 3) observes,

"The concept of pluralism hasn't got any roots in Cambodia. The opposition is almost by definition disloyal."

These attitudes become apparent from the speechmaking of Cambodia's long-serving prime minister, Hun Sen. Addressing diplomats and local critics, he intoned, "Those of you who would like to issue

In Cambodia, 'the opposition is almost by definition disloyal'

a statement, both Khmer and foreigners, I would call you stupid, dumb, and ignorant....You only recognize the rights of the opposition, not lawful rights of those in power" (Men 2009). In giving

warning to civil society activists, he advised, "I only need two hours to take over all of Phnom Penh. If you want to try, from this hour, I only need two hours, not longer than that, to grab you all" (ibid). In commenting on democracy's prospects, he remarked, "The shortcut is the people power. In Cambodia, you cannot do that....Do not provoke the problem. No matter how big you are, I will handcuff you" (Yun 2008a). And in defending the social functionality of patronage, he asked, "Will corrupt officials agree to any confiscation of their riches? No. Then war will erupt. After confiscating for awhile, all the rich people will all become poor, as in Khmer Rouge times, more than three million people will be destroyed. Don't play with that" (Guthrie 2008).

After the founding election in 1993, Hun Sen ascended to the prime ministership through intense maneuvering. Over time, he fused his party, the Cambodian People's Party (CPP), with the state apparatus, enabling him to freely access and distribute public resources. As single-party dominance was imposed, democracy contracted into a base form of electoral authoritarianism. Freedom of communication has thus been constrained, with the government controlling all radio and television broadcasting. But owing to low literacy rates, less consistent control has been exercised over the print media, thereby enabling critical commentary to surface. Even so, during the CPP's tenure, journalists have occasionally been killed, most recently Khim Sambor, who wrote for the local newspaper *Khmer Conscience* on electoral cheating, land grabbing, and illegal logging (Thayer 2009: 87). More routinely, the government used its grip on the judiciary to bring lawsuits for defamation, misinformation, and incitement against its critics, leading to arrests and jail terms. In 2008, the editor of *Khmer*

Conscience, Dam Sith, was arrested on defamation charges after publishing an opposition party's allegations that government ministers had ties to the Khmer Rouge. In 2009, Hang Chakra, the publisher of *Khmer Machas Srok,* also affiliated with the opposition, was imprisoned for defamation. The editor-in-chief, Chum Sophal, advised that "for security reasons and the longevity of the newspaper, we are reducing the number of articles that criticize the government. Otherwise, the government will charge us and we will have to close the newspaper." Lim Kayhong, publisher of *New Liberty News,* stated similarly: "My newspaper is afraid of the government in the current situation.... The situation is not good for us because if we are strong [against the government], we will share the fate of Hang Chakra and Dam Sith" (Yun and Lindsay 2009).

Freedom of assembly has also been stifled in Cambodia, as the government has suppressed protests mounted by workers over low wages in foreign-invested garment industries and by farmers over the loss of their land to developers, who are frequently linked to the CPP. Recently, the government imposed legislation that requires organizers to announce their demonstrations five days in advance and to limit their events to 200 persons. New statutes have also restricted demonstrations in Phnom Penh to a single venue, christened "Freedom Park," which is located far from the National Assembly and key public edifices.

On the regime's electoral dimension, the CPP has continued to hold multiparty elections, but severely manipulated their procedures. It has packed the National Election Committee with loyalists, made free use of government workers and facilities during campaigning, and resorted regularly to intimidation. However, in elections held in 1993, 1998, and 2003, the CPP either lost to its monarchial rival, Funcinpec (National United Front for an Independent, Neutral, Peaceful, and Cooperative Cambodia), or failed to win decisively enough to rule alone. Thus, only by pressuring Funcinpec to coalesce as a subordinate partner, a strategy that in the late 1990s produced great violence, was Hun Sen able to hold the prime ministership. With civil liberties so sharply contained and elections so deeply manipulated, Freedom House (2010) has long given Cambodia a low score of 5 for civil liberties and 6 for political rights, and designated the country as "not free."

However, by 2008, with rapid economic growth driven by construction, agriculture, and garment exports, the CPP began to find favor among trade unions and rural populations. Availing itself of the bureaucratic conduits that it had constructed and the public resources it accumulated, the party ordered wage increases for factory workers and funded development projects for farmers. In the country's most recent election, then, held in 2008, CPP won by such enlarged majorities that it might even have governed alone.

Accordingly, with elections legitimating rather than threatening its hold on state power, the CPP has continued to wage them. As Duncan McCargo (2005: 100) writes, Hun Sen has sought an "outward show of electioneering to legitimize the status quo." Thus, while the CPP has steadily marginalized the royalist Funcinpec, the prime minister has tolerated a newer opposition vehicle, the reformist Sam Rainsy Party (SRP). Its founder, Sam Rainsy, a middle-class professional who once ran an accountancy firm in Paris, returned to Cambodia for the 1993 election, contesting as a candidate for Funcinpec. He then served as finance minister in the ruling coalition that was formed with the victorious CPP. However, in seeking to increase tax collection and reduce corruption, Rainsy drew "a storm of protest from the entrenched business and political elite" (St. John 2005: 416). He was ousted from the cabinet in 1994, and expelled from Funcinpec and the Assembly in 1995.

The Cambodian People's Party uses an 'outward show of electioneering to legitimize the status quo'

In organizing the SRP, Rainsy appealed strongly to the country's small middle class and its ranks of factory workers. In the 2003 election, his party eclipsed a wilting Funcinpec, winning 24 of the 123 seats in the National Assembly. And in the 2008 election, the SRP increased its seat total to 26. However, the capacity of the opposition to impose accountability has remained scant. As Fish and Kroenig (2009: 112) observe:

> The legislature enjoys some clout through its formally specified prerogatives and some institutional capacity, but it is still largely subordinate to Hun Sen and his Cambodian People's Party (CPP). The legislature's control over, and autonomy from, Hun Sen are severely limited....The legislature has little ability to oversee the government, and its institutional

autonomy is circumscribed by executive decree, dissolution, and impoundment powers.

Nonetheless, Fish and Kroenig assign the National Assembly a surprisingly robust PPI score of .59, ranking it even more highly that Indonesia's DPR and the Philippine Congress. But this must be ascribed to the Assembly's formally recorded powers, rather than the opposition's ability to make use of them effectively in checking the executive. Indeed, Ronald St. John (2005: 416) rightly characterizes the body as "little more than a rubber stamp."

Thus, while opposition parties have won as much as one-fifth of the National Assembly's seats, Hun Sen has stoutly resisted any checks of his abuses. In particular, he has needed little information from the legislature about elite-level patronage that horizontal accountability can provide. Rather, by placing many of his family members in positions of influence, whether through direct appointment or marriage, he has established alternative mechanisms for feedback. As Bertil Lintner (2007) records, Hun Sen's daughter is married to the son of his "right-hand man," the minister of the Council of Ministers; his brother is a provincial governor; his son is married to the daughter of the national police commissioner; and a second son is married to the daughter of the secretary of state for rural development. Other elites, including the chairman of the National Assembly, Heng Samrin, have likewise forged family networks. Instead of seeking information about patronage, Hun Sen has sought legitimacy from the Assembly, which has encouraged him to tolerate its activities, albeit at low levels.

Hun Sen has established feedback mechanisms by placing his family members in positions of influence

Even so, the SRP has labored to use the limited tools at hand to impose accountability. To be sure, with the party under relentless pressure from the government, it has suffered defections (Thayer 2009: 88). The SRP, as well as those parties associated with it, has been refused any broader inclusion in the government's coalition. As the information minister, Kheu Kanhartih, warned unequivocally after the CPP's electoral victory in 2008, "any parties that ally themselves with

William Case

the SRP will not be able to join with the ruling party" (Yun 2008b). Accordingly, those members who remain in opposition have been unmotivated by any hopes of government favor and patronage. Rather, the middle-class professionals and NGO leaders who form the SRP's core have sought steadfastly to advance democratic change by checking the executive. One important example involves the party's secretary general, Mu Sochua, who joined the party after resigning as minister of women's affairs in 2004 in order to protest the government's corruption. In this way, she quickly emerged as "the most prominent woman in Cambodia's struggling political opposition" (Mydans, 2010).

In striving to impose accountability, the SRP has made use of various strategies, both within the Assembly and outside the chamber. Exploiting its prerogatives granted in Article 94 of the Constitution, it has tried to set up a select commission to probe the government over its handling of border issues. Further, though it has little prospect of blocking the government's bills, it has challenged them vigorously during debates and question time. The SRP joined with the newly formed Human Rights Party (HRP), which won three seats in the 2008 election, to fiercely contest the law on demonstrations that limits the number of protesters. And in leading the opposition, Sam Rainsy declared passionately on the floor:

> We have said that we need peace. If we are lying in a grave, things are nice and quiet, but no one wants "grave peace." We want the peace of an active society. We want a security of freedom, the security of people who live with full rights—not the security of slaves.

Rainsy was then roundly denounced by CPP members for having "sullied the debate with 'insults'" that denigrated even the king (Meas 2009a). Nonetheless, the opposition parties persevered in demanding that nearly half of the bill's articles be amended.

Further, when the government recently drafted a bill establishing a "modern" penal code, Mu Sochua welcomed its provisions that outlawed the forging of documents, noting coyly that they could be used to punish "powerful people" who, armed with fake titles, pushed farmers from their land. But she bitterly criticized those sections that appeared to make it even easier for the government to file lawsuits over "public defamation" and "insulting officials." Members of the opposition demanded again that amendments be made. But in this instance, the chairman closed the Assembly's doors, hence barring the United Nations human rights observers who regularly attend its debates, citing "procedural problems in the admission of visitors." The Assembly's live television feed was also cut, which the government attributed to "technical hitches" (Johnston 2009b: 6). The bill was then quickly passed by a large majority. Adopting a tactic used by the opposition in Malaysia, the SRP and HRP duly walked out.

Members of the opposition have also gathered in front of the National Assembly building to voice their discontent, sometimes dramatizing their actions by wearing masks. The SRP has drawn attention too by regularly holding press conferences and circulating critical newsletters and position papers. When Hang Chakra, the publisher of *Khmer Machas Srok*, was jailed for defamation, a delegation of opposition members gained an audience with the king to seek his intervention. It used the occasion also "to report on the legislature's recent activities" (Meas 2009b). Further, in turning the tables on the government, Mu Sochua filed a defamation suit against Hun Sen for sexual discrimination after he had publicly disparaged her as a "strong leg," a demeaning term in Cambodia for a woman.

The opposition parties have also challenged election returns. After the 2008 contest, the SRP and the HRP jointly rejected the results, alleging that the government had tampered with voter lists. The SRP made some 150 complaints to the Electoral Committee at the commune level, then lodged appeals and further complaints with the committee at the national level, as well as with the Constitutional Council. After its complaints were rejected by the Council, the SRP forwarded them to relevant offices in the United Nations and the European Union. Sam Rainsy and the HRP leader, Kem Sokha, also took up their complaints with the leaders of countries involved in Cambodia's 1991 peace agreement, and made visits to Brussels and Paris.

As the swearing-in ceremony for the fourth National Assembly approached, the SRP and the HRP threatened to boycott. In this way, they seemed to win concessions from Hun Sen, including his agreement to acknowledge "the official role of the opposition and opposition leader," to provide budgetary support for the chamber, and to respect legislative immunity. Although the opposition members attended the ceremony, they displayed their continuing grievances by refusing to wear the traditional dress uniform (Thayer 2009: 91).

After the National Assembly convened, the government rapidly filled its cabinet positions by renewing its incumbent ministers and deputy ministers. But it also appointed some 35 defectors from the SRP as secretaries and undersecretaries, giving substance to its co-optative strategies. In addition, though opposition parties had in the past chaired as many as two of the Assembly's nine committees, the CPP this time laid claim to all the top posts. Anticipating the CPP's "block voting" that rammed such decisions through, the SRP and HRP boycotted the Assembly's opening session (Thayer 2009: 91).

More generally, in appealing to popular discontent, Sam Rainsy has variously tarred CPP leaders as either associated with the dreaded Khmer Rouge or in cahoots with the locally maligned Vietnamese. On a more positive tack, the SRP has tirelessly petitioned international organizations over the government's restrictions on civil liberties, its manipulating elections, and its violating human rights. And as noted above, opposition party leaders have travelled frequently to Europe and the United States to make their case to international leaders and émigré Khmer communities.

> *Opposition leaders in Cambodia tirelessly petition international organizations, but to little avail*

But under Cambodia's rigorous form of single-party dominance and electoral authoritarian rule, the government has rebuffed or ignored even these modest attempts to impose accountability. Notwithstanding Hun Sen's earlier pledge, the Assembly has, at the urging of the courts, gathered in closed-door sessions to strip Sam Rainsy, Mu Sochua, and other opposition members of their legislative immunity, hence exposing them to defamation charges. Indeed, Hun Sen responded to Mu Sochua's suit against him, which the courts dismissed, by counter-suing both Mu and her lawyer for defamation. Hun Sen also silenced the Cambodian Confederation of Unions as it prepared to protest in support of Mu, threatening, "I'll use the means of a thorn pitted against a thorn" (Heng 2009). Further, in early 2010, with Sam Rainsy's immunity having again been lifted, he was sentenced in absentia to two years in prison for having pulled up markers on the Cambodia-Vietnam border, therein "inciting discrimination." Later in 2010, he was sentenced to an additional ten years for having posted a "fake map" of the border area on his party's website, hence disseminating "disinformation." While this ruling will likely encourage Rainsy to remain overseas in exile, a SRP spokesman, Yim Sovann, characterized it as "a huge setback for democracy in Cambodia" (*South China Morning Post* 2010b).

In sum, Cambodia's government, in taking a base approach to electoral authoritarianism, has sought legitimating cover for its interminable tenure rather than any information about elite-level patronage flows. As McCargo (2005: 100) stresses, "Elections in Hun Sen's Cambodia have become an exercise in political theater that the CPP uses to legitimize its power." But in responding to pressures for vertical accountability through wage increases and development spending, the government feels even less need for horizontal accountability in the Assembly today, encouraging it further to hound the opposition. However, so long as the electoral authoritarian regime features even a slight legislative aperture through which to check the executive, what stands out is an opposition still motivated to use it.

Singapore

Singapore operates an electoral authoritarian regime that, like Cambodia's, is narrowly constrained. The government curbs freedom of speech and the press through its vigilant deployment of the judiciary and its tireless lodging of defamation suits. It also limits freedom of assembly. The country's Parliament passed legislation in 2009 requiring police permission for all public gatherings, which had previously been required only for gatherings of five or more (Freedom House 2010). It is thus difficult to imagine in Singapore's setting anything like the protests and rallies that were mounted in neighboring Malaysia during 2007–2008.

But it is on the electoral dimension, with the rules over contestation heavily manipulated, that Singapore most visibly slips below Malaysia to the bottommost rung of the electoral authoritarian category. Though multiparty elections for the country's Parliament are regularly held, the opposition is hobbled by the government's many formal restrictions and implicit

Singapore slips below Malaysia to the bottommost rung of the electoral authoritarian category

threats. In joining opposition parties, politicians risk severe forms of harassment, including investigations, disqualification, interference in their livelihoods, and even detention. Further, among a great range of barriers to campaigning, they confront the Group Representative Constituencies (GRC), a scheme whereby all parties contesting in a particular district must run a slate of four to six candidates who have been recruited from each of the country's designated ethnic communities. Launched in 1988 and steadily expanded afterward, GRCs are now in place in more than half the districts. Opposition parties are effectively barred from fielding candidates, given the burden of the GRC requirements and the scantiness of their own resources and membership bases.

Further, in seeking entry to Parliament, though the opposition parties still manage collectively to attract as much as 40 percent of the popular vote, their ranks are so winnowed by a single-member district plurality system that they typically capture very few of the legislature's 70–80 seats. In 1984, the opposition parties were so popular among young voters in the new middle class, as well as ethnic Chinese voters in the working class, that, for the first time, they gained two seats in Parliament. In 1991, they raised their total to four. Thereafter, the government, in its alarm, grew "much less tolerant of democratic processes and more willing to exercise its extraordinary powers in a vindictive manner against its critics" (Means 1995: 109). Accordingly, Singapore's civil liberties are rated at 4 and its political rights at 5 by Freedom House (2010) today. And as its "legislature's powers are few and scattered" (Fish and Kroenig 2009: 590), its PPI score stands at a lowly .38.

Thus, while opposition leaders in Singapore are fabled for their personal sacrifices, their negligible presence in Parliament has prevented their imposing any horizontal accountability. The government has foregone the informational benefits that, under electoral authoritarianism, a legislature motivated to check the executive can provide. Of course, Singapore's small set of elites remains

Singapore's small set of elites is tightly embedded in the ruling party and state bureaucracy

tightly integrated, often by kinship or marriage, across peak positions in the ruling People's Action Party (PAP), the state bureaucracy, key enterprises styled locally as Government Linked Corporations (GLCs), leading academic institutions, and the military apparatus. The government has remained intimately aware, then, of the privileged networks through which high-level appointments and rewards are shared (Barr 2006).

Beginning in the 1980s, then, the government also sought information about the preferences of ordinary citizens. It formed the Feedback Unit through which to engage the new middle class, as well as corporate mechanisms and support programs that embraced industrial workers. But its insights into middle-class expectations and labor grievances remained incomplete. Many middle-class citizens, uplifted through Singapore's unique mode of state capitalism, have shown new interest in questions over the environment, gender inequity, cultural expression, and sexuality. The PAP has shied away from many of these issues for fear of alienating working-class majorities. However, the PAP's programmatic appeals and trade union formations have also failed to entice those workers who have been battered by intense globalization. Thus, while Boix and Svolik (n.d.) maintain that governments operating electoral authoritarian regimes can gain information about elite-level activities through the legislature, Singapore's government has used Parliament to learn more about social forces.

Accordingly, with opposition members nearly absent from the legislature, the government has molded surrogates since the early 1990s, installing a bloc of as many as nine Nominated Members of Parliament (NMPs). Through an applications process involving screening by a select parliamentary committee and approval by the president, NMPs are given terms of up to two-and-a-half years. They are recruited from among senior position holders in business, the legal and medical professions, and academia,

> *With opposition nearly absent in Singapore's parliament, the government has taken to molding a surrogate*

but also from the National Trade Union Congress women's groups and minority and cultural associations. The NMP scheme was intended to secure nonpartisan "experts." But its proposal in 1989 met with "exceptional controversy." Hence, the coldness with which its early cohorts were received by the government's many elected MPs—made anxious about the erosion of their "own status as representatives" (Rodan 2009: 444–45)—has evoked a semblance of proxy opposition.

Though hard to measure, it is unlikely that this NMP scheme generates perceptions of legitimacy or even much representativeness among middle-class and working-class citizens. Unelected, NMPs have gained no consent from any constituency. And unlike ordinary elected MPs, they are unable to vote on money bills, proposed constitutional amendments, or no-confidence motions (Rodan 2009: 444). Nonetheless, in operating under electoral authoritarianism, they have gathered in a form of opposition. Undistracted by thoughts of material patronage, yet doubtless valuing the social accolades that their parliamentary service elicits, some NMPs have grown motivated to use what latitude they possess to hold the government accountable for its inattention to middle-class youths and workers.

In this way, the government has gained some new insights. For example, during the Eighth Parliament, an orthopedic surgeon and ardent feminist, Kanwaljit Soin, "dominated parliamentary question time…and shaped public debate" (Rodan 2009: 449). And though the Family Violence Bill that she introduced was finally voted down, some of its provisions were incorporated by the government into its Women's Charter. In the Ninth and Tenth Parliaments, a television show host and winner of the 2006 Youth Award, Eunice Olsen, addressed a wide variety of issues, including "GLC accountability" (Rodan 2009: 451–52, 457). In these same Parliaments, Siew Kum Hong championed gay rights, seeking to repeal existing legislation in order to decriminalize homosexuality.

The extent to which the government has benefited from the information generated by the NMPs, strengthening its standing and perpetuating its regime, is hard to assess. Rodan (2009: 442) is himself imprecise over the scheme's functional impact, at different times citing its rationale as "technocratic governance," "political co-option," and the "strategic inclusion of…emerging social forces." Either way, the usefulness of even the low-level accountability that the NMPs have imposed is evinced by the government's investing so many resources in its institutionalization. As Rodan (2009: 457) observes, several NMPs had been invited directly by ministers to apply for positions, signifying "the importance the government attaches to this new category of appointments."

Conclusions

This analysis began with an assumption that what matters most for imposing accountability is a legislature that features a sharply demarcated and motivated opposition. But it also drew upon Fish and Kroenig's less obvious claim that in structuring supportive dynamics between the executive and legislature, overarching institutional design counts for little. Whether in a presidential system, such as in Indonesia or the Philippines, or a parliamentary system, as in Thailand, legislatures have failed to effectively check the executive. However, analysis found no evidence for Fish and Kroenig's next contention that more crucial than formal institutional design were actual legislative powers, measurable on their Parliamentary Powers Index. Put simply, in Southeast Asia, weakly endowed legislatures have tried more consistently than strong ones to check the executive.

By way of explanation, data from Southeast Asia indicate that more central for accountability than either institutional design or legislative powers is a country's broader regime type, which determines how motivated legislators are to use what powers they possess. In most developing countries, a large literature demonstrates that the surest route to accumulating wealth lies in accessing public resources. In a new democracy, businesspeople and professionals regularly seek election to the legislature, hoping to bolster

> *Regime type, more than institutional design or legislative power, is crucial for holding the executive accountable*

their stakes. After gaining entry, their pursuits may be ordered by networking elites based either in resilient political parties, as in Indonesia, or quite disposable vehicles, as in the Philippines. Alternatively, relations may be strained by rival elites, whether grounded in a two-party system (like under Thaksin Shinawatra in Thailand, however lopsided) or an amorphous array of multiple parties (like in Thailand prior to Thaksin). But whether accommodative or fractious, members of legislatures in new democracies have been unswerving in their prioritizing patronage over horizontal accountability. Indeed, in rare instances where they did impose accountability, they sought principally to wring additional patronage from the executive. On the other side, executives resist such accountability, as their submitting to it on a vertical dimension through elections has already earned them substantial legitimacy.

Under electoral authoritarianism, most members of the legislature remain equally geared to patronage. But analysis shows that the leadership paramountcy and single-party dominance that typically underpin electoral authoritarian regimes exclude a minority of members, barring their parties from the ruling coalition and denying them patronage. Hence, in entering the legislature with different motivations, these members cohere in sharp opposition, seeking to expose the executive's abuses in hopes of galvanizing citizens

> *Under electoral authoritarianism, legislators can better impose accountability in part because the executive may insist on it*

and advancing democratic change. At the same time, the executive may tolerate this, calculating that through the controls electoral authoritarianism affords, he or she can obscure the abuses that come to light. Thus, with electoral manipulations having stunted vertical accountability, the executives in Malaysia and, in some measure, in Cambodia have gauged that the deficits in legitimacy can be remedied by cautiously submitting to the legislature's horizontal accountability. In a weaker manifestation of this dynamic, Singapore's executive has also fostered some horizontal accountability, though less to fill legitimacy deficits than information gaps about the policy preferences of new social forces.

Fluctuations in the political records of these three countries provide evidence from new angles, then, upon which to draw conclusions about electoral authoritarianism's dynamics. In Malaysia, as the election in 2008 carried the opposition closer to power and drove the regime nearer to democracy, some of the opposition's newly recruited members in the state-level governments that it now controlled withdrew from the horizontal accountability to which their parties were committed and focused their attention on seeking state contracts. Their activities highlighted in another way, then, the causal links between regime types and the motivational logic of legislatures: while electoral authoritarianism stiffens the opposition and strengthens horizontal accountability, the opposition's rise leads it to hunt for patronage.

In Cambodia, by contrast, with the government funding development programs that boosted its legitimacy, the corresponding gains that it made in the 2008 election led to a reduction of its already limited tolerance for opposition. This adjustment underscored the links between regime types and the calculations often made by the executive: while electoral authoritarianism encourages the government to permit some horizontal accountability, any new burst of electoral success may tempt it more heavily to dampen the opposition.

Under conditions of electoral authoritarianism, then, Malaysia demonstrates how a surging opposition may shift its ambitions from imposing horizontal accountability to pursuing patronage. And Cambodia shows how an invigorated government may change in its behaviors from tolerating accountability to waging repression. By contrast, Singapore's record indicates that while electoral authoritarianism may come under strain, it can also be renewed. In Singapore, the opposition has made none of the gains that its counterpart has in Malaysia. And its government has won legitimation through economic expansion for much longer than its counterpart in Cambodia. But in valuing the information that small infusions of horizontal accountability can deliver, the government has rekindled some of the opposition that it had nearly extinguished. Singapore thus reminds us that a legislature can better impose accountability under electoral authoritarianism than in a new democracy, in part because the executive may insist on it.

But how might these trajectories, so disappointing for democracy's advocates, be significantly altered? Many ordinary recommendations might be rehearsed about the need to strengthen political parties. Organizational apparatuses must be better elaborated and made more durable. Social bases must be charged with ideological appeals and programmatic commitments. But at root there lies the need for much more dramatic shifts in the motivational logic by which members of legislatures are guided, the drivers of which are unclear. As this analysis has shown, institutional design matters little. Further, the vigilant civil society that is often evoked, though it may hasten a transition to democracy through momentous popular upsurge, finds its attention waning amid the tedium of functional consolidation. And the democracy promotion in which international agencies have invested so heavily has produced only modest effects.

In the near term, then, it is hard to imagine that the motivations of members of legislatures can be changed. But over time, the modernization upon which so many social prescriptions hinge may have salubrious political impact. By vitalizing markets and creating alternative avenues of wealth creation, the attractiveness of legislatures as sites of enrichment will shrink. Persons seeking election to legislatures will be less geared to patronage than to performing legislative tasks, including imposing accountability. And the executive, noting the availability of private-sector positions to which to repair, may submit more readily to the oversight that constrains public office. We conclude, then, that democracy may consolidate best when it is not the only game in town.

> *As markets are vitalized, legislatures will shrink as attractive sites of personal enrichment*

Endnotes

1. The work described in this paper was fully supported by a grant from the Research Grants Council of the Hong Kong Special Administrative Region, China (Project No. 9041396).

2. Fieldwork in support of this project on legislative functioning in Southeast Asia involved extensive interviewing of representatives, legislature officials, NGO members, and local academics and journalists. Interviewing was conducted in Kuala Lumpur, Malaysia, in December 2008; in Jakarta, Indonesia, in June 2009; and in Manila and Quezon City, the Philippines, in August 2010. The vast majority of respondents requested anonymity as a condition for granting interviews. This was especially true for legislative officials like chiefs-of-staff and their subordinates, commission and committee staff officials, and legislative researchers—although it was usually these respondents who provided the greatest insights and information. As one congressional staff member noted candidly during an interview at the House of Representative complex in Constitution Hills, Quezon City, the Philippines, "I don't always like what I see here. I try to be professional. But it is not advisable to speak out." Where respondents did not object, however, their names and titles are recorded in the text.

Bibliography

Abinales, Patricio N. 2008. "The Philippines: Weak State, Resilient President." In Singh, Daljit, and Tin Maung Maung Than, eds. 2008. *Southeast Asian Affairs* 2008. Singapore: ISEAS, 293–312.

Asia Sentinel. 2009. "Scandal Threatens Indonesia's Reform Agenda," September 4, at http://www.asiasentinel.com/index.php?option=com_content&task=view &id=2039&Itemid=175.

———. 2010a. "Indonesia Bailout Farce Appears Over," March 4, at http://www .asiasentinel.com/index.php?option=com_content&task=view&id=2326 &Itemid=377.

———. 2010b. "Indonesia's Bakrie Grabs New Post," May 12, at http://www.asiasentinel .com/index.php?option=com_content&task=view&id=2455&Itemid=175.

Aspinall, Edward. 2005. *Opposing Suharto: Compromise, Resistance, and Regime Change in Indonesia.* Stanford: Stanford University Press.

———. 2010. "Indonesia: The Irony of Success." *Journal of Democracy* 21(2): 20–34.

Barkan, Joel D. 2009. "African Legislatures and the 'Third Wave' of Democratization," in Joel D. Barkan, ed., *Legislative Power in Emerging African Democracies.* Boulder: Lynne Reinner.

Barr, Michael. 2006. "Beyond Technocracy: The Culture of Elite Governance in Lee Hsien Loong's Singapore." *Asian Studies Review* 30(1): 1–17.

Beh Lih Yi. 2006. "I Asked Customs to Close One Eye: Jasin MP," *Malaysiakini*, May 4, at http://www.malaysiakini.com/news/50630.

———. 2008a. "Khairy's 'Planted' NEP Question Causes a Stir," *Malaysiakini*, May 15, at http://malaysiakini.com/news/82903.

———. 2008b. "MACC: Good Enough for BN; Pakatan Wants Improvement," *Malaysiakini*, December 15, at http://www.malaysiakini.com/news/94902.

———. 2008c. "BN MPs: JAC 'Against Spirit of Constitution,'" *Malaysiakini*, December 17, at http://www.malaysiakini.com/news/95032.

Bima Arya Sugiarto. 2006. "Entrepreneurs Are Transforming Political Parties," *Inside Indonesia*, July-September, 34.

Boix, Carles, and Milan Svolik. n.d. "The Foundations of Limited Authoritarian Government: Institutions and Power-sharing in Dictatorships," at https://netfiles.uiuc.edu/msvolik/www/research/institutions.pdf.

Bordadora, Norman. 2007. "De Venecia Calls on Arroyo to Set Up New Administration," *Inquirer.net*, October 18, at http://newsinfo.inquirer.net/breakingnews/nation/view/20071018-95153/De_Venecia_calls_on_Arroyo_to_set_up_new_administration.

———— and Nikko Dizon. 2007. "Solon Cites Many Trips to China for Golf, Sex," *Philippine National Inquirer*, August 30, at http://frjessie.wordpress.com/2007/08/.

Boudreau, Vince. 2010. "Elections, Repression and Authoritarian Survival in Post-Transition Indonesia and the Philippines." In Case, William, ed. 2010. *Contemporary Authoritarianism in Southeast Asia: Structures, Institutions, and Agency*. Milton Park: Routledge.

Brownlee, Jason. 2007. *Authoritarianism in an Age of Democracy*. Cambridge: Cambridge University Press.

Cambodia News. 2008. "Cambodia Using 'Subtle' Intimidation, Sam Rainsy," June 20, at http://camboda.com/news.php?gcm=7011&gnid=8126.

Case, William. 2010. "Transitions from Single-party Dominance: New Data from Malaysia." *Journal of East Asian Studies* 10(1): 91–126.

Chin, James, and Wong Chin Huat. 2009. "Malaysia's Electoral Upheaval." *Journal of Democracy* 20(3): 71–85.

Committee on Accountability of Public Officers and Investigations (Blue Ribbon Committee). 2009. *NBN-ZTE Scandal*, November 11, at http://www.senate.gov.ph/publications/CR%202009-01%20-%20Committee%20Report%20743.pdf.

Committee on Justice. 2005. *Committee Report No. 1012: Impeachment Proceedings Against President Gloria Macapagal-Arroyo*. Quezon City: House of Representatives, Republic of the Philippines.

————. 2008. *Committee Report No. 1551: Impeachment Proceedings Against President Gloria Macapagal-Arroyo*. Quezon City: House of Representatives, Republic of the Philippines.

Conde, Carlos H. 2008. "Allies of Arroyo Force Out Philippine House Speaker," *International Herald Tribune*, February 6, 3.

Coronel, Sheila. 2004. "How Representative Is Congress?" Philippines Center for Independent Journalism, March, at www.pcij.org/stories/2004/congress.html.

Crouch, Harold. 1996. *Government and Society in Malaysia*. Ithaca: Cornell University Press.

De Venecia Jr., Jose. 2007. "Forward," *House of Representatives Final Performance Report, 13th Congress*, July.

Diamond, Larry. 1999. *Developing Democracy: Toward Consolidation.* Baltimore: Johns Hopkins University Press.

———, Marc F. Plattner, and Andreas Schedler. 1999. "Introduction." In Schedler, Andreas, Larry Diamond, and Marc F. Plattner, eds. 1999. *The Self-Restraining State: Power and Accountability in New Democracies.* Boulder: Lynne Rienner.

Ding, Jo-Ann. 2010. "Assessing Pakatan Rakyat in Selangor," *The Nut Graph,* September 20, at http://www.thenutgraph.com/assessing-pakatan-rakyat-in-selangor/.

Dzulkefly Ahmad. 2010. "Pakatan Rakyat Needs to Get Its Act Together." July 29, at http://blog.drdzul.com/2010/07/29/pakatan-rakyat-needs-to-get-its-act-together/.

Economist. 2010. "After a Hard-Won Battle, President Yudhoyono Has a Chance to Start Again," March 6, 29.

Emmerson, Donald K. 2004. "Indonesia's Approaching Elections: A Year of Voting Dangerously?" *Journal of Democracy* 15(1): 94–108.

Financial Times. 2010. "Indonesia Warned of Opposition to Reform," May 26, 10.

Fish, M. Steven. 2006. "Creative Constitutions: How Do Parliamentary Powers Shape the Electoral Arena?" In Schedler, Andreas, ed. 2006. *Electoral Authoritarianism: The Dynamics of Unfree Competition.* Boulder: Lynne Rienner.

——— and Matthew Kroenig. 2009. *The Handbook of National Legislatures: A Global Survey.* Cambridge: Cambridge University Press.

Freedom House. 2006. *Freedom in the World 2006—Philippines,* at http://www.freedomhouse.org/inc/content/pubs/fiw/inc_country_detail.cfm?year=2006&country=7039&pf.

———. 2010. *Freedom in the World 2010: Erosion of Freedom Intensifies,* at http://www.freedomhouse.org/uploads/fiw10/FIW_2010_Tables_and_Graphs.pdf.

Fuzi Omar, Muhamad. See Muhamad Fuzi Omar.

Gandhi, Jennifer, and Adam Przeworski. 2006. "Cooperation, Cooptation, and Rebellion Under Dictatorships," *Economics and Politics* 18(1): 1–26.

Geddes, Barbara. 1999. "What Do We Know About Democratization After Twenty Years?" *Annual Review of Political Science* 2: 115–144.

GMA News. 2008. "Hello Garci Scandal," January 25, at http://www.gmanews.tv/story/27477/Hello-Garci-scandal.

GMA News. 2009a. "SONA 2009: Fast Facts on the House of Representatives," at http://images.gmanews.tv/pdf/SONA%202009--House%20of%20Representatives%20fast%20facts.pdf.

———. 2009b. "Looking Back: The NBN-ZTE Controversy," August 29, at http://www.gmanews.tv/story/171031/looking-back-the-nbn-zte-controversy.

Gomez, Edmund Terence, and K.S. Jomo. 1999. *Malaysia's Political Economy: Politics, Patronage, and Profits.* Cambridge: Cambridge University Press.

Guthrie, Craig. 2008. "Towards Hun Sen's Cambodia," *Asia Times*, July 23, at http://www.atimes.com/atimes/Southeast_Asia/JG23Ae01.html.

Heng Reaksmey. 2009. "Hun Sen Warns Against Opposition Rally," *VOANews.com*, June 17, at http://www.voanews.com/Khmer-english/news/a-40-2009-06-17-voa8-90170212.html.

House of Representatives, Republic of the Philippines. 2009. *14th Congress, Second Regular Session: Accomplishment Report*, July 2008–2009, at http://www.congress.gov.ph/download/14th/2009_accrep_second.pdf.

———. n.d. *Priority Development Assistance Fund: House of Representatives*, at http://www.congress.gov.ph/pdaf/index.php.

Hughes, Caroline. 2009. "Cambodia in 2008: Consolidation in the Midst of Crisis." *Asian Survey* 49(1): 206–212.

Human Rights Watch. 2010. "Cambodia: Opposition Leader Sam Rainsy's Trial a Farce," January 28, at http://www.hrw.org/en/news/2010/01/28/cambodia-opposition-leader-sam-rainsy-s-trial-farce.

Huntington, Samuel P. 1991. *The Third Wave: Democratization in the Late Twentieth Century*. Norman: University of Oklahoma Press.

Hutchcroft, Paul D. 1998. *Booty Capitalism: The Politics of Banking in the Philippines*. Ithaca: Cornell University Press.

———. 2000. "Colonial Masters, National Politicos and Provincial Lords: Central Authority and Local Autonomy in the American Philippines, 1900–1913." *Journal of Asian Studies* 59(2): 277–306.

———. 2007. "Countries at the Crossroads 2007: Country Report—Philippines," Freedom House, at http://www.freedomhouse.org/modules/publications/ccr/modPrintVersion.cfm?edition=8&ccrpage=37&ccrcountry=165.

———. 2008. "The Arroyo Imbroglio in the Philippines," *Journal of Democracy* 19(1): 141–55.

Ilagan, Karol, and Malou Mangahas. 2009. "Conflicted Contracts: Firms Linked to 4 Legislators, Governor, Awarded Projects," Philippine Center for Investigative Journalism (PCIJ) May 1, at http://pcij.org/stories/contractors-linked-to-four-legislators-governor-awarded-dpwh-projects/.

Irawaty Wardany. 2009. "Court Lengthens Sentences for Two Legislators," *Jakarta Post*, April 4, at http://www.thejakartapost.com/news/2009/04/04/court-lengthens-sentences-two-legislators.html.

Jakarta Globe. 2009. "Ex-Lawmaker Handed Three-Year Sentence in Rp 3b Corruption Case," October 30, at http://www.thejakartaglobe.com/national/ex-lawmaker-handed-three-year-sentence-in-rp-3b-corruption-case/338738.

———. 2010. "Megawati's Family 'Not Divided' Over Deputy Post," March 31, at http://www.thejakartaglobe.com/national/megawatis-family-not-divided-over-deputy-post/366963.

Jakarta Post. 2010. "Dozens of PDI-P Politicians Receive Briberies: Prosecutors," March 8, at http://www.thejakartapost.com/news/2010/03/08dozens-pdip-politicians-receive-briberies-prosecutors.html.

Jesudason, James V. 1989. *Ethnicity and the Economy: The State, Chinese Business, and Multinationals in Malaysia.* Singapore: Oxford University Press.

Johnston, Tim. 2009a. "Rash of Lawsuits Sees Cambodia Crack Down on Dissenters," *Financial Times,* July 27, 3.

———. 2009b. "Cambodia Accused of Using Law to Stifle Protests," *Financial Times,* October 22, 6.

Juwono, Vishnu, and Sebastian Eckardt. 2008. "Budget Accountability and Legislative Oversight in Transition: The Case of Post-Suharto Indonesia." In Stapenhurst, Rick, Riccardo Pelizzo, David M. Olson, and Lisa von Trapp, eds. 2008. *Legislative Oversight and Budgeting: A World Perspective.* Washington, DC: The World Bank.

Kim Quek. 2008. "PM's 'Reform Bills' Mere Humbug?" *Malaysiakini,* December 19, at http://www.malaysiakini.com/news/95119.

Laver, Michael, and Kenneth A. Shepsle. 1999. "Government Accountability in Parliamentary Democracy." In Przeworski, Adam, Susan C. Stokes, and Bernard Manin, eds. 1999. *Democracy, Accountability, and Representation.* Cambridge: Cambridge University Press.

League of Provinces of the Philippines. 2008. "Govs Call on Senate to Stop NBN Probe," February, at http://www.1pp.gov.ph/ph/fe b08-news1.html.

Lintner, Bertil. 2007. "One Big Happy Family in Cambodia," *Asia Times Online,* March 20, at http://www.atimes.com/atimes/Southeast_Asia/IC20Ae03.html.

Linz, Juan J., and Alfred Stepan. 1996. *Problems of Democratic Transition and Consolidation: Southern Europe, South America, and Post-Communist Europe.* Baltimore: Johns Hopkins University Press.

Lust, Ellen. 2009. "Competitive Clientelism in the Middle East." *Journal of Democracy* 20(3): 122–35.

Mauzy, Diane. 1993. "Malaysia: Malay Political Hegemony and 'Coercive Consociationalism." In McGarry, John, and Brendan O'Leary, eds. 1993. *The Politics of Ethnic Conflict Regulation.* New York: Routledge.

McCargo, Duncan. 2005. "Cambodia: Getting Away with Authoritarianism?" *Journal of Democracy* 16(4): 98–112.

Means, Gordon. 1995. "Soft Authoritarianism in Malaysia and Singapore," *Journal of Democracy* 7(4): 103–117.

Meas Sokchea. 2009a. "National Assembly Reports Debate on Demonstration Law," *Phnom Penh Post,* October 20, at http://www.phnompenhpost.com/index .php/2009102029057/National-news/national-assembly-reopens-debate -on-demonstration-law.html.

———. 2009b. "SRP Pursues King's Help to Free Editor," *Phnom Penh Post,* October 28, at http://ki-media.blogspot.com/2009/10/srp-pursues-kings-help-to -free-editor.html.

Melendez, Carlos. 2009. "Dataset Review: Parliamentary Powers Index," *APSA-CP Newsletter* 20(2): 19–22.

Melia, Thomas O. 2010. "What Makes Legislatures Strong?" *Journal of Democracy* 21(2): 166–72.

Men Kimseng. 2009. "Lawmaker Worried Over Recent Hun Sen Remarks," *VOANews. com*, August 14, at http://khmernz.blogspot.com/2009/08/lawmaker -worried-over-recent-hun-sen.html.

Mietzner, Marcus. 2008. "Comparing Indonesia's Party Systems of the 1950s and the Post-Suharto Era: From Centrifugal to Centripetal Inter-Party Competition." *Journal of Southeast Asian Studies* 39(3): 431–53.

————— and Edward Aspinall. 2010. "Problems of Democratisation in Indonesia: An Overview." In Aspinall, Edward, and Marcus Mietzner, eds. 2010. *Problems of Democratisation in Indonesia: Elections, Institutions and Society.* Singapore: ISEAS.

Muhamad Fuzi Omar. 2008. "Parliamentary Behaviour of the Members of Opposition Political Parties in Malaysia." *Intellectual Discourse* 16(1): 21–48.

Mydans, Seth. 2010. "Crusader Rowing Upstream in Cambodia," *New York Times*, February 22, at http://www.nytimes.com/2010/02/22/world/asia/22cambowomen .html.

Nograles, Prospero C., and Edcel C. Lagman. n.d. "Understanding the 'Pork Barrel,'" at http://www.congress.gov.ph/pdf/pork_barrel.pdf.

Noore Alam Siddiquee. 2006. "Paradoxes of Public Accountability in Malaysia: Control Mechanisms and Their Limitations." *International Public Management Review* 7(2): 43–64.

O'Donnell, Guillermo. 1998. "Horizontal Accountability in New Democracies." In *Journal of Democracy* 9(3): 112–26.

Ordenes-Cascolan, Lala. 2007. "Congress Passes Even Fewer Laws on Bigger Budget," April 23, at http://pcij.org/i-report/2007/13thcongress.html.

Pelizzo, Riccardo, and Bernize Ang. 2008. "An Ethical Map of Indonesian MPs." *Public Integrity* 10(3): 253–72.

Pepinsky, Thomas B. 2007. "Malaysia: Turnover Without Change." *Journal of Democracy* 18(1): 113–127.

Philippines Center for Independent Journalism. 2004a. "De Venecia's Reign Is Challenged," July 26, at www.pcij.org/stories/2004/house.html.

—————. 2004b. "Representatives Scramble for Power, Peso and Privilege," July 27, at http://pcij.org/stories/representatives-scramble-for-power-peso-and-privilege.

Philippines Country Management Unit. 2005. *Country Assistance Strategy for the Philippines, 2006–2008.* Washington, DC: World Bank.

Quimpo, Nathan. 2009. "The Philippines: Predatory Regime, Growing Authoritarian Features." *Pacific Review* 22(3): 335–53.

Rakner, Lise, and Nicolas van de Walle. 2009. "Opposition Weakness in Africa." *Journal of Democracy* 20(3): 108–21.

Rodan, Garry. 2009. "New Modes of Political Participation and Singapore's Nominated Members of Parliament." *Government and Opposition* 44(4): 438–62.

St. John, Ronald Bruce. 2005. "Democracy in Cambodia—One Decade, US$5 Billion Later: What Went Wrong?" *Contemporary Southeast Asia* 27(3): 406–28.

Salaverria, Leila B. 2010. "At Palace or House, Arroyo Under Heavy Fire," *Inquirer.net*, August 3, at http://newsinfo.inquirer.net/inquirerheadlines/nation/view/20100803-284608/At-Palace-or-House-Arroyo-under-heavy-fire.

Schedler, Andreas. 2002. "The Nested Game of Democratization by Elections." *International Political Science Review* 23(1): 103–122.

———. 2010. "Authoritarianism's Last Line of Defense." *Journal of Democracy* 21(1): 70–80.

Schneier, Edward. 2004. "Emerging Patterns of Legislative Oversight in Indonesia." In Pelizzo, Riccardo, Rich Stapenhurst, and David Olson, eds. 2004. *Trends in Parliamentary Oversight*. Washington, DC: The International Bank for Reconstruction and Development/The World Bank.

Sebastian, Leonard C. 2004. "The Paradox of Indonesian Democracy." *Contemporary Southeast Asia* 26(2): 256–79.

Sherlock, Stephen. 2007. "The Indonesian Parliament after Two Elections: What Has Really Changed?" Centre for Democratic Institutions, January, at www.cdi.anu.edu.au.

———. 2009. "Indonesia's 2009 Elections: The New Electoral System and Competing Parties," Centre for Democratic Institutions, January, at www.cdi.anu.edu.au.

———. 2010. "The Parliament in Indonesia's Decade of Democracy: People's Forum or Chamber of Cronies?: In Aspinall, Edward, and Marcus Mietzner, eds. 2010. *Problems of Democratisation in Indonesia: Elections, Institutions and Society*. Singapore: ISEAS.

Slater, Dan. 2004. "Indonesia's Accountability Trap: Party Cartels and Presidential Power after Democratic Transition." *Indonesia* 78, October, 61–92.

Social Watch Philippines. 2009. "House Committee on Appropriations Supports Campaign for 2010 Alternative Budget," October 4, at http://www.socialwatchphilippines.org/news_14_committee%20on%20appro.htm.

South China Morning Post. 2010a. "Reformers Face Criminal Probe," March 4, A8.

———. 2010b. "Sam Rainsy Given 10-year Term for Map," September 24, A10.

Stepan, Alfred, and Cindy Skach. 1993. "Constitutional Frameworks and Democratic Consolidation: Parliamentarism versus Presidentialism." *World Politics* 46(1): 1–22.

Tan, Kimberly Janet T. 2010. "Mikey Arroyo, Bro. Mike Nominees of Party-list Groups," GMANews.TV, March 23, at http://www.gmanews.tv/story/186846/mikey-arroyo-bro-mike-nominees-of-party-list-groups.

Thayer, Carlyle A. 2009. "Cambodia: The Cambodian People's Party Consolidates Power." In Singh, Daljit, ed. 2009. *Southeast Asian Affairs 2009*. Singapore: ISEAS.

Thompson, Mark R. 1995. *The Anti-Marcos Struggle: Personalistic Rule and Democratic Transition in the Philippines*. New Haven: Yale University Press.

Tomas, Dirk. 2010. "The Party System after the Elections: Towards Stability?" In Aspinall, Edward, and Marcus Mietzner, eds. 2010. *Problems of Democratisation in Indonesia: Elections, Institutions and Society.* Singapore: ISEAS.

Ubac, Michael Lim. 2007. "Arroyo Takes Country on Tour of Super Regions," *Inquirer.net,* July 24, at http://newsinfo.inquirer.net/inquirerheadlines/nation /view/200707724-78335/Arroyo_takes_country_on_tour_of_super_regions#

—— and Edson C. Tandoc Jr. 2009. *Inquirer.net,* August 29, at http://www.inquirer. net/specialfeatures/nbndeal/archive.php?pageID=2.

Ufen, Andreas. 2006. *Political Parties in Post-Suharto Indonesia: Between Politik Aliran and 'Philippinisation.'* Hamburg: German Institute of Global and Area Studies Working Papers, no. 37.

von Luebke, Christian. 2010. "The Politics of Reform: Political Scandals, Elite Resistance, and Presidential Leadership in Indonesia." *Journal of Current Southeast Asian Affairs* 29(1): 79–94.

Wall Street Journal. 2009. "Indonesia Dilutes Antigraft Court," September 30, at http://online.wsj.com/article/SB125423653353249493.html.

Wright, Joseph. 2008. "Do Authoritarian Institutions Constrain? How Legislatures Affect Economic Growth and Investment." *American Journal of Political Science* 52(2): 322–43.

Yun Samean. 2008a. "PM: Anti-Gov't Rallies Will Be Met with Force," *The Cambodia Daily,* April 15, at http://www.camnet.com.kh/cambodia.daily/selected_ features/cd-Apr-15-2008.htm.

——. 2008b. "Four Parties Reject Results of 'Rigged' Election," *Cambodia Daily,* July 29, at http://www.camnet.com.kh/cambodia.daily/selected_features/cd-Jul-29-2008. htm.

—— and Bethany Lindsay. 2009. "Opposition Newspapers Losing Their Bite," *Cambodia Daily,* July 17, at http://www.camnet.com.kh/cambodia.daily /selected_features/cd-Jul-17-2009.htm.

Zakaria Haji Ahmad. 1989. "Malaysia: Quasi-Democracy in a Divided Society." In Diamond, Larry, Juan J. Linz, and Seymour Martin Lipset, eds. 1989. *Democracy in Developing Countries: Asia.* Boulder: Lynne Rienner.

Ziegenhain, Patrick. 2008. *The Indonesian Parliament and Democratization.* Singapore: Institute of Southeast Asian Studies.

Policy Studies series

A publication of the East-West Center

Series Editors: *Edward Aspinall and Dieter Ernst*
Publications Coordinator: *Carol Wong*

Description
Policy Studies provides policy-relevant scholarly analysis of key contemporary domestic and international issues affecting Asia. The editors invite contributions on Asia's economics, politics, security, and international relations.

Notes to Contributors
Submissions may take the form of a proposal or complete manuscript. For more information on the Policy Studies series, please contact the Series Editors.

Editors, *Policy Studies*
East-West Center
1601 East-West Road
Honolulu, Hawai'i 96848-1601
Tel: 808.944.7197
Publications@EastWestCenter.org
EastWestCenter.org/policystudies

www.ingramcontent.com/pod-product-compliance
Lightning Source LLC
Chambersburg PA
CBHW050554280326
41933CB00011B/1833